Federal Laws Relating to Cybersecurity: Discussion of Proposed Revisions

Eric A. Fischer

Senior Specialist in Science and Technology

June 29, 2012

Congressional Research Service

7-5700

www.crs.gov

R42114

CRS Report for Congress

Prepared for Members and Committees of Congress

Summary

For more than a decade, various experts have expressed increasing concerns about cybersecurity, in light of the growing frequency, impact, and sophistication of attacks on information systems in the United States and abroad. Consensus has also been building that the current legislative framework for cybersecurity might need to be revised.

The complex federal role in cybersecurity involves both securing federal systems and assisting in protecting nonfederal systems. Under current law, all federal agencies have cybersecurity responsibilities relating to their own systems, and many have sector-specific responsibilities for critical infrastructure.

More than 50 statutes address various aspects of cybersecurity either directly or indirectly, but there is no overarching framework legislation in place. While revisions to most of those laws have been proposed over the past few years, no major cybersecurity legislation has been enacted since 2002.

Recent legislative proposals, including many bills introduced in the 111th and 112th Congresses, have focused largely on issues in 10 broad areas (see "Selected Issues Addressed in Proposed Legislation" for an overview of how current legislative proposals would address issues in several of those areas):

- national strategy and the role of government,

- reform of the Federal Information Security Management Act (FISMA),

- protection of critical infrastructure (including the electricity grid and the chemical industry),

- information sharing and cross-sector coordination,

- breaches resulting in theft or exposure of personal data such as financial information,

- cybercrime,

- privacy in the context of electronic commerce,

- international efforts,

- research and development, and

- the cybersecurity workforce.

For most of those topics, at least some of the bills addressing them have proposed changes to current laws. Several of the bills specifically focused on cybersecurity have received committee or floor action, but none have become law.

Comprehensive legislative proposals on cybersecurity that have received considerable attention in 2012 are S. 2105, recommendations from a House Republican task force, and a proposal by the Obama Administration. They differ in approach, with S. 2105 proposing the most extensive regulatory framework and organizational changes of the three, and the task force recommendations focusing more on incentives for improving private-sector cybersecurity. An alternative to S. 2105, S. 3342 (a refinement of S. 2151), does not include enhanced regulatory authority or new federal entities, but does include cybercrime provisions.

Several narrower House bills have been introduced that address some of the issues raised and recommendations made by the House task force. Four passed the House the week of April 23:

- Cybersecurity Enhancement Act of 2011 (H.R. 2096), which addresses federal cybersecurity R&D and the development of technical standards;

- Cyber Intelligence Sharing and Protection Act (H.R. 3523), which focuses on information sharing and coordination, including sharing of classified information;

- Advancing America's Networking and Information Technology Research and Development Act of 2012 (H.R. 3834), which addresses R&D in networking and information technology, including but not limited to security; and

- Federal Information Security Amendments Act of 2012 (H.R. 4257), which addresses FISMA reform.

One was ordered reported out of the full committee but did not come to the floor:

- Promoting and Enhancing Cybersecurity and Information Sharing Effectiveness Act of 2011 or PRECISE Act of 2011 (H.R. 3674), which addresses the role of the Department of Homeland Security in cybersecurity, including protection of federal systems, personnel, R&D, information sharing, and public/private sector collaboration in protecting critical infrastructure;

Together, those House and Senate bills address most of the issues listed above, although in different ways. All include proposed revisions to some existing laws covered in this report.

Contents

Tables

Contacts

Introduction

For more than a decade, various experts have expressed concerns about information-system security—often referred to as *cybersecurity*—in the United States and abroad.[1] The frequency, impact, and sophistication of attacks on those systems has added urgency to the concerns.[2] Consensus has also been growing that the current legislative framework for cybersecurity might need to be revised to address needs for improved cybersecurity, especially given the continuing evolution of the technology and threat environments. This report, with contributions from several CRS staff (see **Acknowledgments**), discusses that framework and proposals to amend more than 30 acts of Congress that are part of or relevant to it. For a CRS compilation of reports and other resources on cybersecurity, see CRS Report R42507, *Cybersecurity: Authoritative Reports and Resources*, by Rita Tehan. For additional selected CRS reports relevant to cybersecurity, see CRS Issues in Focus: *Cybersecurity*.

Current Legislative Framework

The federal role in addressing cybersecurity is complex. It involves both securing federal systems and fulfilling the appropriate federal role in protecting nonfederal systems. There is as yet no overarching framework legislation in place, but many enacted statutes address various aspects of cybersecurity. Some notable provisions are in the following acts:

---

[1] The term *information systems* is defined in 44 U.S.C. §3502 as "a discrete set of information resources organized for the collection, processing, maintenance, use, sharing, dissemination, or disposition of information," where *information resources* is "information and related resources, such as personnel, equipment, funds, and information technology." Thus *cybersecurity,* a broad and arguably somewhat fuzzy concept for which there is no consensus definition, might best be described as measures intended to protect information systems—including technology (such as devices, networks, and software), information, and associated personnel—from various forms of attack. The concept has, however, been characterized in various ways. For example, the interagency Committee on National Security Systems has defined it as "the ability to protect or defend the use of cyberspace from cyber attacks," where *cyberspace* is defined as "a global domain within the information environment consisting of the interdependent network of information systems infrastructures including the Internet, telecommunications networks, computer systems, and embedded processors and controllers" (Committee on National Security Systems, *National Information Assurance (IA) Glossary*, April 2010, http://www.cnss.gov/Assets/pdf/cnssi_4009.pdf). In contrast, cybersecurity has also been defined as synonymous with *information security* (see, for example, S. 773, the Cybersecurity Act of 2010, in the 111th Congress), which is defined in current law (44 U.S.C. §3532(b)(1)) as

> protecting information and information systems from unauthorized access, use, disclosure, disruption, modification, or destruction in order to provide—
>
> > (A) integrity, which means guarding against improper information modification or destruction, and includes ensuring information nonrepudiation and authenticity;
> > (B) confidentiality, which means preserving authorized restrictions on access and disclosure, including means for protecting personal privacy and proprietary information;
> > (C) availability, which means ensuring timely and reliable access to and use of information; and
> > (D) authentication, which means utilizing digital credentials to assure the identity of users and validate their access.

[2] See, for example, IBM, *IBM X-Force® 2011 Mid-year Trend and Risk Report*, September 2011, http://public.dhe.ibm.com/common/ssi/ecm/en/wgl03009usen/WGL03009USEN.PDF; Barbara Kay and Paula Greve, *Mapping the Mal Web IV* (McAfee, September 28, 2010), http://us mcafee.com/en-us/local/docs/MTMW_Report.pdf; Office of the National Counterintelligence Executive, *Foreign Spies Stealing U.S. Economic Secrets in Cyberspace: Report to Congress on Foreign Economic Collection and Industrial Espionage, 2009-2011*, October 2011, http://www.ncix.gov/publications/reports/fecie_all/Foreign_Economic_Collection_2011.pdf; Symantec, *Symantec Internet Security Threat Report: Trends for 2010*, Volume 16, April 2011, https://www4.symantec.com/mktginfo/ downloads/21182883_GA_REPORT_ISTR_Main-Report_04-11_HI-RES.pdf.

- *The Counterfeit Access Device and Computer Fraud and Abuse Act of 1984* prohibits various attacks on federal computer systems and on those used by banks and in interstate and foreign commerce.

- *The Electronic Communications Privacy Act of 1986 (ECPA)* prohibits unauthorized electronic eavesdropping.

- *The Computer Security Act of 1987* gave the National Institute of Standards and Technology (NIST) responsibility for developing security standards for federal computer systems, except the national security systems[3] that are used for defense and intelligence missions, and gave responsibility to the Secretary of Commerce for promulgating security standards.

- *The Paperwork Reduction Act of 1995* gave the Office of Management and Budget (OMB) responsibility for developing cybersecurity policies.

- *The Clinger-Cohen Act of 1996* made agency heads responsible for ensuring the adequacy of agency information-security policies and procedures, established the chief information officer (CIO) position in agencies, and gave the Secretary of Commerce authority to make promulgated security standards mandatory.

- *The Homeland Security Act of 2002 (HSA)* gave the Department of Homeland Security (DHS) some cybersecurity responsibilities in addition to those implied by its general responsibilities for homeland security and critical infrastructure.

- *The Cyber Security Research and Development Act,* also enacted in 2002, established research responsibilities in cybersecurity for the National Science Foundation (NSF) and NIST.

- *The E-Government Act of 2002* serves as the primary legislative vehicle to guide federal IT management and initiatives to make information and services available online, and includes various cybersecurity requirements.

- *The Federal Information Security Management Act of 2002 (FISMA)* clarified and strengthened NIST and agency cybersecurity responsibilities, established a central federal incident center, and made OMB, rather than the Secretary of Commerce, responsible for promulgating federal cybersecurity standards.

More than 40 other laws identified by CRS also have provisions relating to cybersecurity (see **Table 2**). Revisions to many of those laws have been proposed. More than 40 bills and resolutions with provisions related to cybersecurity have been introduced in the 112th Congress, including several proposing revisions to current laws. In the 111th Congress, the total was more

---

[3] This term is defined in 44 U.S.C. §3542(b)(2).

than 60.[4] Several bills in both Congresses received committee or floor action, but none have become law. In fact, no comprehensive cybersecurity legislation has been enacted since 2002.[5]

Executive Branch Actions

Some significant executive actions have been taken, however.[6] The George W. Bush Administration established the Comprehensive National Cybersecurity Initiative (CNCI) in 2008 through National Security Presidential Directive 54 / Homeland Security Presidential Directive 23 (NSPD-54/HSPD-23). Those documents are classified, but the Obama Administration released a description of them in March 2010.[7] Goals of the 12 subinitiatives in that description include consolidating external access points to federal systems; deploying intrusion detection and prevention systems across those systems; improving research coordination and prioritization and developing "next-generation" technology, information sharing, and cybersecurity education and awareness; mitigating risks from the global supply chain for information technology; and clarifying the federal role in protecting critical infrastructure.

In December 2009, the Obama Administration appointed Howard Schmidt to the position of White House Cybersecurity Coordinator.[8] He is a member of the White House national security staff and is responsible for government-wide coordination of cybersecurity, including the CNCI. One of the most visible initiatives in which he has been involved is the implementation of automated, continuous monitoring of federal information systems.[9] Other stated priorities include developing a unified strategy for network security and incident response, and strengthening partnerships with the private sector and other countries. He works with both the National Security and Economic Councils in the White House. However, the position has no direct control over agency budgets, and some observers argue that operational entities such as the National Security

---

[4] Those bills were identified through a two-step process—candidates were found through searches of the Legislative Information System (LIS, http://www.congress.gov) using "cybersecurity," "information systems," and other relevant terms in the text of the bills, followed by examination of that text in the candidates to determine relevance for cybersecurity. Use of other criteria may lead to somewhat different results. For example, using the LIS "cybersecurity" topic search yields about 30 bills in the 112th Congress and 40 in the 111th, with about a 50% overlap in the bills included. While that difference is higher than might be expected, none of the bills identified uniquely by the LIS topic search are relevant to the discussion in this report.

[5] Among the broader proposals in the 111th Congress, S. 773 (S.Rept. 111-384) and S. 3480 (S.Rept. 111-368) were reported by the originating committees. H.R. 4061 (H.Rept. 111-405) and H.R. 5136 (Title XVII, mostly similar to H.R. 4900) both passed the House. A bill combining provisions of the two Senate bills was drafted (Tony Romm, "Lack of Direction Slows Cybersecurity," *Politico*, November 4, 2010, http://www.politico.com/news/stories/1110/44662.html). In the 112th Congress, S. 413 is similar to S. 3480 in the previous Congress, H.R. 2096 (H.Rept. 112-264) is similar to H.R. 4061, and the Senate combined bill, S. 2105, includes elements of S. 773, S. 413, S. 2102, and a proposal put forward by the White House in April 2011 (see below).

[6] This update does not include executive branch actions taken since December 2011.

[7] The White House, "The Comprehensive National Cybersecurity Initiative," March 5, 2010, http://www.whitehouse.gov/cybersecurity/comprehensive-national-cybersecurity-initiative. For additional information about this initiative and associated policy considerations, see CRS Report R40427, *Comprehensive National Cybersecurity Initiative: Legal Authorities and Policy Considerations*, by John Rollins and Anna C. Henning.

[8] The position has been popularly called the "cyber czar."

[9] Jeffrey Zients, Vivek Kundra, and Howard A. Schmidt, "FY 2010 Reporting Instructions for the Federal Information Security Management Act and Agency Privacy Management," Office of Management and Budget, Memorandum for Heads of Executive Departments and Agencies M-10-15, April 21, 2010, http://www.whitehouse.gov/omb/assets/memoranda_2010/m10-15.pdf.

Agency (NSA) have far greater influence and authority.[10] The Obama Administration has also launched several initiatives.[11]

Under current law, all federal agencies have cybersecurity responsibilities relating to their own systems, and many have sector-specific responsibilities for critical infrastructure, such as the Department of Transportation for the transportation sector. Cross-agency responsibilities are complex, and any brief description is necessarily oversimplified. In general, in addition to the roles of White House entities, DHS is the primary civil-sector cybersecurity agency. NIST, in the Department of Commerce, develops cybersecurity standards and guidelines that are promulgated by OMB, and the Department of Justice is largely responsible for the enforcement of laws relating to cybersecurity.[12] The National Science Foundation (NSF), NIST, and DHS all perform research and development (R&D) related to cybersecurity. The National Security Agency (NSA) is the primary cybersecurity agency in the national security sector, although other agencies also play significant roles. The recently established U.S. Cyber Command, part of the U.S. Strategic Command in the Department of Defense (DOD), has primary responsibility for military cyberspace operations.

Legislative Proposals

In general, legislative proposals on cybersecurity in the 111th and 112th Congresses have focused largely on issues in 10 broad areas:

- national strategy and the role of government,

- reform of FISMA,

- protection of critical infrastructure (especially the electricity grid and the chemical industry),

- information sharing and cross-sector coordination,

- breaches resulting in theft or exposure of personal data such as financial information,

- cybercrime offenses and penalties,

- privacy in the context of electronic commerce,

- international efforts,

- research and development (R&D), and

---

[10] See, for example, Seymour M. Hersh, "Judging the cyber war terrorist threat," *The New Yorker*, November 1, 2010, http://www.newyorker.com/reporting/2010/11/01/101101fa_fact_hersh?currentPage=all.

[11] Among them are White House strategies to improve the security of Internet transactions (The White House, *National Strategy for Trusted Identities in Cyberspace*, April 2011, http://www.whitehouse.gov/sites/default/files/rss_viewer/ NSTICstrategy_041511.pdf) and to coordinate international efforts (The White House, *International Strategy for Cyberspace*, May 2011, http://www.whitehouse.gov/sites/default/files/rss_viewer/ international_strategy_for_cyberspace.pdf), and an executive order on sharing and security for classified information (Executive Order 13587, "Structural Reforms to Improve the Security of Classified Networks and the Responsible Sharing and Safeguarding of Classified Information," *Federal Register* 76, no. 198 (October 13, 2011): 63811-63815, http://www.gpo.gov/fdsys/pkg/FR-2011-10-13/pdf/2011-26729.pdf).

[12] This responsibility is shared to some extent with other agencies such as the U.S. Secret Service.

- the cybersecurity workforce.

For most of those topics, at least some of the bills addressing them proposed changes to current laws.[13]

Selected Legislative Proposals in the 112th Congress

There appears to be considerable support in principle for significant legislation to address most of those issues. The House, Senate, and White House have taken somewhat different approaches to such legislation.

The Senate has been working since last year on a comprehensive bill synthesizing approaches proposed by the Homeland Security and Governmental Affairs Committee (S. 3480 in the 111th Congress and S. 413 in the 112th), the Commerce, Science, and Transportation Committee (S. 773 in the 111th Congress), and others. S. 2105, the Cybersecurity Act of 2012, which includes features of both those bills and others,[14] was introduced in February 2012. An alternative Senate bill, S. 3342, the SECURE IT Act,[15] is a revision of S. 2151, which was originally introduced in March.[16] Several other Senate bills would address specific aspects of cybersecurity, such as data breaches of personal information and cybercrime.

In April 2011, the White House sent a comprehensive, seven-part legislative proposal (*White House Proposal*) to Congress.[17] Some elements of that proposal have been included in both House and Senate bills.

In October, the 12-Member House Republican Cybersecurity Task Force, which had been formed by Speaker Boehner in June, released a series of recommendations (*Task Force Report*) to be used by House committees in developing cybersecurity legislation.[18] Unlike the other proposals, it was not presented in the form of a bill or bills. Several House bills have been introduced subsequently that address some of the issues raised and recommendations made by the *Task Force Report.* Four passed the House the week of April 23:

- Cybersecurity Enhancement Act of 2011 (H.R. 2096), which would addresses federal cybersecurity R&D and the development of technical standards;

---

[13] For specific analysis of legal issues associated with several of the bills being debated in the 112th Congress, see CRS Report R42409, *Cybersecurity: Selected Legal Issues*, by Edward C. Liu et al.

[14] The title on information sharing is similar to S. 2102.

[15] SECURE IT is an acronym for Strengthening and Enhancing Cybersecurity by Using Research, Education, Information and Technology.

[16] A very similar but not identical bill, H.R. 4263, was introduced in the House April 9. It is not discussed separately in this update.

[17] The White House, *Complete Cybersecurity Proposal*, 2011, http://www.whitehouse.gov/sites/default/files/omb/legislative/letters/law-enforcement-provisions-related-to-computer-security-full-bill.pdf. One part does not appear to be directly related to cybersecurity. It would restrict the authority of state and local jurisdictions with respect to the location of commercial data centers.

[18] House Republican Cybersecurity Task Force, *Recommendations of the House Republican Cybersecurity Task Force*, October 5, 2011, http://thornberry.house.gov/UploadedFiles/CSTF_Final_Recommendations.pdf.

- Cyber Intelligence Sharing and Protection Act (H.R. 3523), which focuses on information sharing and coordination, including sharing of classified information;[19]

- Advancing America's Networking and Information Technology Research and Development Act of 2012 (H.R. 3834), which addresses R&D in networking and information technology, including but not limited to security;[20] and

- Federal Information Security Amendments Act of 2012 (H.R. 4257), which addresses FISMA reform.

A fifth bill was ordered reported out of full committee on April 18 but was not included in the cybersecurity bills debated on the House floor the week of April 23:[21]

- Promoting and Enhancing Cybersecurity and Information Sharing Effectiveness Act of 2011 or PRECISE Act of 2011 (H.R. 3674), which addresses the role of the Department of Homeland Security in cybersecurity, including protection of federal systems, personnel, R&D, information sharing, and public/private sector collaboration in protecting critical infrastructure.

Specific issues addressed by several of those bills and proposals are noted in **Table 1**. Together, they address most of the issues listed above, although in different ways. All include or discuss proposed revisions to some existing laws covered in this report.

Those addressed in the House bills are

- "Cyber Security Research and Development Act, 2002" (H.R. 2096, S. 2105, S. 2151, S. 3342);

- "Federal Information Security Management Act of 2002 (FISMA)" (H.R. 4257, the *Task Force Report*, S. 2105, S. 2151, S. 3342, the *White House Proposal*);

- "High Performance Computing Act of 1991" (H.R. 3834, S. 2105, S. 2151, S. 3342)

- "Homeland Security Act of 2002 (HSA)" (H.R. 3674, S. 2105, the *White House Proposal*); and

- "National Security Act of 1947" (H.R. 3523).

---

[19] The Obama Administration has objected to this bill, claiming that it does not address cybersecurity needs for critical infrastructure, and contains overly broad liability protections for private-sector entities and insufficient protections for individual privacy, confidentiality, and civil liberties (The White House, "H.R. 3523—Cyber Intelligence Sharing and Protection Act," Statement of Administration Policy, April 25, 2012, http://www.whitehouse.gov/sites/default/files/omb/legislative/sap/112/saphr3523r_20120425.pdf). The Administration has not released statements of administration policy for any of the other bills discussed in this report.

[20] For discussion of this bill and H.R. 2096, see also CRS Report RL33586, *The Federal Networking and Information Technology Research and Development Program: Background, Funding, and Activities*, by Patricia Moloney Figliola.

[21] H.R. 3674 was marked up by the Subcommittee on Cybersecurity, Infrastructure Protection, and Security Technologies of the Committee on Homeland Security on February 1 and forwarded to the full committee, which substantially amended the bill in its April 18 markup.

Table 1. Comparison of Topics Addressed by Selected Legislative Proposals on Cybersecurity in the 112ᵗʰ Congress

Topic	Selected House Bills	Task Force Report	S. 2105	S. 3342 (S. 2151)	White House Proposal
DHS authorities for protection of federal systems	H.R. 3674	X	X		X
New DHS office/center	H.R. 3674		X		X
Cybersecurity workforce authorities and programs	H.R. 2096 H.R. 3674 H.R. 3834	X	X	X	X
Supply-chain vulnerabilities	H.R. 3674	X	X		X
Cybersecurity R&D	H.R. 2096 H.R. 3674 H.R. 3834	X	X	X	X
FISMA reform	H.R. 4257	X	X	X	X
Protection of privately held critical infrastructure (CI)	H.R. 3674	X	X		X
Government/private-sector collaboration on CI protection	H.R. 3674	X	X		X
Additional regulation of privately held critical infrastructure		X	X		X
Information sharing	H.R. 3523 H.R. 3674	X	X	X	X
FOIA exemption for cybersecurity information	H.R. 3523	X	X	X	X
New information-sharing entities	(H.R. 3674)ᵃ	X	X		
Public awareness	H.R. 2096	X	X		X
Cybercrime law		X		X	X
Data breach notification		X			X
Internet security provider code of conduct		X			
National security/defense and federal civil sector coordination		X			

Source: CRS.

Note: S. 3342 is a revised version of S. 2151.

a. The subcommittee version of this bill would have created a new nonprofit quasi-governmental information-sharing entity, but the committee version omitted those provisions (see "Information Sharing").

Those addressed in other legislative proposals are

- "Antitrust Laws and Section 5 of the Federal Trade Commission Act" (*Task Force Report*, S. 2151, S. 3342)

- "Clinger-Cohen Act (Information Technology Management Reform Act) of 1996" (S. 2105, *White House Proposal*);[22]

- "Counterfeit Access Device and Computer Fraud and Abuse Act of 1984" (*Task Force Report*, S. 2151, S. 3342, *White House Proposal*);

- "E-Government Act of 2002" (*White House Proposal*);

- "Electronic Communications Privacy Act of 1986 (ECPA)" (*Task Force Report*);

- "Identity Theft Penalty Enhancement Act" (*Task Force Report*); and

- "Racketeer Influenced and Corrupt Organizations Act (RICO)" (*Task Force Report*).

Also, some legislative proposals would provide exemptions under the "Freedom of Information Act (FOIA)" for certain kinds of information provided to the federal government (*Task Force Report,* H.R. 3523, S. 2105, S. 2151, S. 3342, *White House Proposal*). H.R. 3523, S. 2151, and S. 3342 would also permit information sharing that might otherwise be subject to antitrust or other restrictions on sharing,[23] and the *Task Force Report* states that an antitrust exemption might be necessary.

Selected Issues Addressed in Proposed Legislation

The proposals listed in **Table 1** take a range of approaches to address issues in cybersecurity. The discussion below compares those approaches for several issues—"DHS Authorities for Protection of Federal Systems," the "Cybersecurity Workforce," "Research and Development," "FISMA Reform," "Protection of Privately Held Critical Infrastructure (CI)," and "Information Sharing." For discussion of legal issues associated with protection of federal systems, critical infrastructure, and information sharing, see CRS Report R42409, *Cybersecurity: Selected Legal Issues*, by Edward C. Liu et al.

DHS Authorities for Protection of Federal Systems

DHS currently has very limited statutory responsibility for the protection of federal information systems. The degree to which its role should be modified has been a matter of some debate. Five of the legislative proposals listed in **Table 1** address DHS authorities for federal civil systems.[24] All five bills would enhance DHS authorities, although to varying degrees and in varying ways.

The *Task Force Report* proposes that Congress "formalize" DHS's current coordinating role in cybersecurity. H.R. 3674 would add new provisions on DHS cybersecurity activities to Title II of

---

[22] See also "Federal Information Security Management Act of 2002 (FISMA)."

[23] See CRS Report R42409, *Cybersecurity: Selected Legal Issues* for more detail.

[24] As used here, *civil systems* means federal information systems other than national security systems (defined in 44 U.S.C. §3542) and mission-critical Department of Defense and Intelligence Community systems (i.e., compromise of those systems "would have a debilitating impact on the mission" of the agencies [see 44 U.S.C. 3543(c)]).

HSA; S. 2105 and the *White House Proposal* would add a new subtitle to HSA. All three proposals would provide specific authorities and responsibilities to DHS for risk assessments, protective capabilities, and operational cybersecurity activities.

S. 2105 would also create a new, consolidated DHS cybersecurity and communications center with a Senate-confirmed director who would be responsible for managing federal cybersecurity efforts; for developing and implementing information-security policies, principles, and guidelines; and other functions, including risk assessments and other activities to protect federal systems. The *White House Proposal* would provide such enhanced authority to the DHS Secretary rather than a new center. However, the *White House Proposal* would require the Secretary to establish a center with responsibilities for protecting federal information systems, facilitating information sharing, and coordinating incident response. H.R. 3674 would establish a DHS center with responsibility for information sharing (see "Information Sharing") and technical assistance, and would authorize DHS to conduct specific activities to protect federal systems, including risk assessments and access to agency information-system traffic.

S. 2151 would not amend the HSA but would provide the Secretary of Homeland Security with new responsibilities under FISMA. S. 3342 omits some of those responsibilities and modifies others (see "FISMA Reform").

Cybersecurity Workforce

Concerns have been raised for several years about the size, skills, and preparation of the federal and private-sector cybersecurity workforce.[25] Six proposals in **Table 1** would address those concerns in various ways:

- Provide additional federal hiring and compensation authorities (*Task Force Report*, H.R. 3674, S. 2105, *White House Proposal*).

- Establish or enhance educational programs for development of next-generation cybersecurity professionals[26] (*Task Force Report*, H.R. 2096, H.R. 3834, S. 2105, S. 2151, S. 3342).

- Assess workforce needs (H.R. 2096, S. 2105, S. 2151, S. 3342).

- Use public/private-sector personnel exchanges (*Task Force Report*, *White House Proposal*).

---

[25] See, for example, CSIS Commission on Cybersecurity for the 44th Presidency, *Securing Cyberspace for the 44th Presidency*, December 2008, http://www.csis.org/tech/cyber/; Partnership for Public Service and Booz Allen Hamilton, *Cyber IN-Security: Strengthening the Federal Cybersecurity Workforce*, July 2009, http://ourpublicservice.org/OPS/ publications/download.php?id=135; CSIS Commission on Cybersecurity for the 44th Presidency, *A Human Capital Crisis in Cybersecurity*, July 2010, http://csis.org/files/publication/ 100720_Lewis_HumanCapital_WEB_BlkWhteVersion.pdf.

[26] This includes providing requirements or statutory authority for existing programs, such as the joint NSF/DHS Scholarship-for Service Program (see Office of Personnel Management, "Federal Cyber Service: Scholarship For Service," n.d., https://www.sfs.opm.gov/; National Science Foundation, *Federal Cyber Service: Scholarship for Service (SFS)*, NSF 08-600, Program Solicitation, December 2, 2008, http://www.nsf.gov/pubs/2008/nsf08600/nsf08600 htm), the NSA/DHS National Centers of Academic Excellence and National Security Agency ("National Centers of Academic Excellence," January 10, 2012, http://www.nsa.gov/ia/academic_outreach/nat_cae/index.shtml), and the U.S. Cyber Challenge (National Board of Information Security Examiners, "US Cyber Challenge," 2012, https://www.nbise.org/uscc).

Research and Development

The need for improvements in fundamental knowledge of cybersecurity and new solutions and approaches has been recognized for well over a decade[27] and was a factor in the passage of the Cybersecurity Research and Development Act in 2002 (P.L. 107-305, H.Rept. 107-355). That law focuses on cybersecurity R&D by NSF and NIST. The Homeland Security Act of 2002, in contrast, does not specifically mention cybersecurity R&D. However, DHS and several other agencies make significant investments in it. About 60% of reported funding by agencies in cybersecurity and information assurance is defense-related (invested by the Defense Advanced Research Projects Agency [DARPA], NSA, and other defense agencies), with NSF accounting for about 15%, NIST, DHS, and DOE 5%-10% each.[28] Seven of the nine legislative proposals in **Table 1** address cybersecurity R&D. Five would establish requirements for R&D on specific topics such as detection of threats and intrusions, identity management, test beds, and supply-chain security. Agencies for which the proposals include provisions specifying research topics or providing funding authorization include

- DHS (H.R. 3674, S. 2105),
- NIST (H.R. 2096, S. 2151, S. 3342),
- NSF (H.R. 2096, S. 2105, S. 2151, S. 3342), and
- Multiagency[29] (H.R. 3834, S. 2105, S. 2151, S. 3342).

The *Task Force Report*, H.R. 2096, H.R. 3834, S. 2105, S. 2151, and S. 3342 address planning and coordination of research among federal agencies through the White House National Science and Technology Council (NSTC) and other entities. The *White House Proposal* does not include any specific R&D provisions but includes cybersecurity R&D among a set of proposed requirements for the Secretary of Homeland Security.

FISMA Reform

The "Federal Information Security Management Act of 2002 (FISMA)" was enacted in 2002. It revised the framework that had been enacted in several previous laws (see **Table 2**). FISMA has been criticized for focus on procedure and reporting rather than operational security, a lack of widely accepted cybersecurity metrics, variations in agency interpretation of the mandates in the act, excessive focus on individual information systems as opposed to the agency's overall information architecture, and insufficient means to enforce compliance both within and across agencies. Five legislative proposals in the 112th Congress (the *Task Force Report*, H.R. 4257, S. 2105, S. 2151, S. 3342, and the *White House Proposal*) would revise FISMA, while retaining much of the current framework:

---

[27] See, for example, National Research Council, *Trust in Cyberspace* (Washington, DC: National Academies Press, 1999), http://www.nap.edu/catalog/6161.html.

[28] The percentages were calculated from data in Subcommittee on Networking and Information Technology Research and Development, Committee on Technology, *Supplement to the President's Budget for Fiscal Year 2013: The Networking and Information Technology Research and Development Program*, February 2012, http://www.nitrd.gov/PUBS%5C2013supplement%5CFY13NITRDSupplement.pdf. The total investment for FY2011 was $445 million. However, agencies may perform additional research not reported as cybersecurity R&D (e.g., some research on software design or high-confidence systems).

[29] For example, through the Director of the Office of Science and Technology Policy (OSTP).

- All five would continue requirements for agency-wide information security programs, annual independent review of security programs, and reports on program effectiveness and deficiencies.

- All include requirements for continuous monitoring of agency systems, including automated monitoring.

- All would retain the responsibility of NIST for development of cybersecurity standards, including compulsory standards. H.R. 4257 would retain OMB's current responsibility for promulgating the standards, whereas S. 2105, S. 2151, S. 3342, and the *White House Proposal* would transfer that responsibility to the Secretary of Commerce.[30]

- H.R. 4257 would also retain OMB's current responsibility for overseeing federal information-security policy and evaluating agency information-security programs. S. 2105 and the *White House Proposal* would transfer authorities and functions for information security policy from OMB to DHS. OMB has already delegated some authorities to DHS administratively,[31] and the *Task Force Report* expresses support for that approach. S. 2151 and S. 3342, in contrast, would transfer that responsibility to the Secretary of Commerce. However, none of the proposals would give the Secretaries of Commerce or Homeland Security authority to approve or disapprove agency information security plans. Only H.R. 4257 would expressly retain OMB's current power to use its financial authority to enforce accountability.

- S. 2105 and the *White House Proposal* would provide new protective authorities to the Secretary of Homeland Security, including intrusion detection, use of countermeasures, access to communications and other system traffic at agencies, as well as the power to direct agencies to take protective actions and, in the case of an imminent threat, to act without prior consultation to protect agency systems. S. 2151 would provide DHS a much more limited role, requiring it to conduct ongoing security analyses using information provided by the agencies. S. 3342 would give that responsibility instead to OMB.

- Only H.R. 4257 would retain the current FISMA provision giving OMB responsibility for ensuring operation of a federal incident center. However, S.

---

[30] This authority had been granted to the Secretary of Commerce under the Clinger-Cohen Act of 1996 (P.L. 104-106) but was transferred to the Director of OMB by the FISMA title in the HSA in 2002 (P.L. 107-296, Sec. 1002, 40 U.S.C. §11331). Note that the version of the Chapter 35 provisions that is currently in effect (Subchapter III) was enacted by the FISMA title in the E-Government Act of 2002 (P.L. 107-347, Title III), but that is not the case for 40 U.S.C. §11331, for which the version in the E-Government Act would have retained the authority of the Secretary of Commerce to promulgate those standards, even though it was enacted after the HSA. The reason for this potentially confusing difference appears to be that (1) the effective date of HSA was later than that of the E-Government Act, and (2) HSA changed 44 U.S.C. Chapter 35 by amending the existing subchapter II, which the E-Government Act explicitly suspended (see also "Federal Information Security Management Act of 2002 (FISMA)").

[31] See Jeffrey Zients, Vivek Kundra, and Howard A. Schmidt, "FY 2010 Reporting Instructions for the Federal Information Security Management Act and Agency Privacy Management," Office of Management and Budget, Memorandum for Heads of Executive Departments and Agencies M-10-15, April 21, 2010, http://www.whitehouse.gov/omb/assets/memoranda_2010/m10-15.pdf; and Peter R. Orszag and Howard A. Schmidt, "Clarifying Cybersecurity Responsibilities and Activities of the Executive Office of the President and the Department of Homeland Security (DHS)," Office of Management and Budget, Memorandum for Heads of Executive Departments and Agencies M-10-28, July 6, 2010, http://www.whitehouse.gov/sites/default/files/omb/assets/memoranda_2010/m10-28.pdf.

2105 and the *White House Proposal* each contain other provisions that would establish centers within DHS that would provide for incident reporting, information sharing, and other cybersecurity activities. S. 2151 and S. 3342, in contrast, contain provisions to facilitate reporting to a number of centers (see "Information Sharing" below).

Protection of Privately Held Critical Infrastructure (CI)

The federal government has identified 18 sectors of critical infrastructure (CI),[32] much of which is owned by the private sector. The federal role in protection of privately held CI has been one of the most contentious issues in the debate about cybersecurity legislation. There appears to be broad agreement that additional actions are needed to address the cybersecurity risks to CI,[33] but there is considerable disagreement about how much, if any, additional federal regulation is required. Four of the proposals in **Table 1** address protection of privately held CI.

Both S. 2105 and the *White House Proposal* would require the Secretary of Homeland Security to

- designate as covered CI those private-sector CI entities for which a successful cyberattack could have debilitating or catastrophic impacts of national significance,[34]

- determine what cybersecurity requirements or frameworks are necessary to protect them,

- determine whether additional regulations are necessary to ensure that the requirements are met,

- develop such regulations in consultation with government and private-sector entities, and

- enforce the regulations.

The regulations proposed by S. 2105 would require CI owners and operators, unless exempted,[35] to certify compliance annually, based on self- or third-party assessments, and would provide civil

---

[32] See Department of Homeland Security, "Critical Infrastructure", May 4, 2012, http://www.dhs.gov/files/programs/gc_1189168948944.shtm; and CRS Report RL30153, *Critical Infrastructures: Background, Policy, and Implementation*, by John D. Moteff.

[33] See, for example, House Committee on Homeland Security, Subcommittee on Cybersecurity, Infrastructure Protection, and Security Technologies, *Examining the Cyber Threat to Critical Infrastructure and the American Economy*, 2011, http://homeland.house.gov/hearing/subcommittee-hearing-examining-cyber-threat-critical-infrastructure-and-american-economy; Stewart Baker, Natalia Filipiak, and Katrina Timlin, *In the Dark: Crucial Industries Confront Cyberattacks* (McAfee and CSIS, April 21, 2011), http://www mcafee.com/us/resources/reports/rp-critical-infrastructure-protection.pdf; and R. E. Kahn et al., *America's Cyber Future: America's Cyber Future: Security and Prosperity in the Information Age* (Center for a New American Security, May 31, 2011), http://www.cnas.org/files/documents/publications/CNAS_Cyber_Volume%20I_0.pdf.

[34] S. 2105 would largely exempt information technology products and services from designation as covered CI and the cybersecurity regulations the bill would authorize.

[35] An entity would be exempted if the Secretary of Homeland Security determined that it was already sufficiently secure or that additional requirements would not substantially improve its security (Sec. 105(c)(4)). The President would also be permitted to exempt an entity from the requirements upon determining that current regulations sufficiently mitigate the risks to the entity (Sec. 104(f)).

---

penalties for noncompliance. The Secretary would also be authorized to perform assessments where risks justify such action.

The *White House Proposal* would require owners and operators of covered entities, unless exempted,[36] to submit and attest to compliance plans, and certify compliance annually. Independent evaluations would be performed on a schedule determined by the Secretary. Civil penalties, shutdown orders, and requirements for use of particular measures would be prohibited as enforcement methods.

The *Task Force Report* recommends that Congress consider targeted and limited additional regulation of highly regulated industries where required to improve cybersecurity, and that existing regulations be streamlined. For most CI, however, the report recommends that Congress adopt a menu of voluntary incentives.[37] It also recommends limitations on liability for entities that comply. S. 2105 and the *White House Proposal* would also limit liability for entities in compliance.

The subcommittee version of H.R. 3674[38] would have amended the HSA to require the Secretary of Homeland Security to perform continuous risk assessments of CI for inclusion annually in the National Infrastructure Protection Plan.[39] It would also have required relevant federal regulatory agencies to review cybersecurity regulations for covered CI (as determined by the Secretary[40]) and fill any gaps using a collection of recognized consensus standards, where applicable, and to work with NIST to develop such standards where necessary. It would have prohibited additional regulatory authority beyond the collected standards.

The full-committee version of H.R. 3674[41] would amend the HSA in a substantially different way from the subcommittee version. It would permit the Secretary to engage in risk assessments and other protective activities with respect to privately held CI only upon request by owners and operators. It would require the Secretary to develop a cybersecurity strategy for CI systems and stipulates that the bill would not provide additional authority to DHS over federal or nonfederal entities.

Information Sharing

Barriers to the sharing of information on threats, attacks, vulnerabilities, and other aspects of cybersecurity—both within and across sectors—have long been considered by many to be a

---

[36] This exemption (Sec. 9(c) in the part of the proposal on CI protection) is similar to the Presidential exemption in S. 2105 (footnote 35) except that the *White House Proposal* would give the authority to the Secretary of Homeland Security.

[37] Among the possibilities discussed are tying adoption of standards to incentives such as grants and streamlined regulation, using tax credits, and facilitating the development of a cybersecurity insurance market.

[38] This is the version approved by voice vote by the Subcommittee on Cybersecurity, Infrastructure Protection, and Security Technologies of the House Committee on Homeland Security on February 1, 2012, and forwarded to the full committee.

[39] See Department of Homeland Security, *National Infrastructure Protection Plan*, 2009, http://www.dhs.gov/xlibrary/assets/NIPP_Plan.pdf.

[40] The criteria in the subcommittee version of H.R. 3674 are generally similar to those in S. 2105 and the *White House Proposal* in that they focus on entities for which successful cyberattack could have major negative impacts. The definitions in the three legislative proposals differ somewhat in emphasis and specificity.

[41] This is the version ordered reported by the Committee on Homeland Security on April 18, 2012.

---

significant hindrance to effective protection of information systems, especially those associated with CI.[42] Examples have included legal barriers, concerns about liability and misuse, protection of trade secrets and other proprietary business information, and institutional and cultural factors—for example, the traditional approach to security tends to emphasize secrecy and confidentiality, which would necessarily impede sharing of information.

Proposals to reduce or remove such barriers, including provisions in bills in **Table 1**, have raised concerns,[43] some of which are related to the purpose of barriers that currently impede sharing. Examples include risks to individual privacy and even free speech and other rights, use of information for purposes other than cybersecurity, such as unrelated government regulatory actions, commercial exploitation of personal information, or anticompetitive collusion among businesses that would currently violate federal law (see "Antitrust Laws and Section 5 of the Federal Trade Commission Act").

Five proposals in **Table 1** have provisions for improving information sharing and addressing privacy and other concerns, with H.R. 2674 amending the HSA and H.R. 3523 amending the National Security Act of 1947:

- *Create entities for information sharing.* S. 2105 would require the Secretary of Homeland Security to establish a process for designating federal and nonfederal information exchanges, including a lead federal exchange responsible for facilitating information sharing among federal and nonfederal entities. The *Task Force Report* recommends establishment of a nongovernmental clearinghouse for sharing cybersecurity information among private-sector and government entities. The subcommittee version of H.R. 3674 would have created such an organization, the National Information Sharing Organization (NISO).[44] However, those provisions were omitted from the committee version, which would instead provide statutory authorization for and specify governance and responsibilities of the DHS National Cybersecurity and Communications Integration Center (NCCIC),[45] which was established administratively in 2009.[46] S. 2151 and S.

---

[42] See, for example, The Markle Foundation Task Force on National Security in the Information Age, *Nation At Risk: Policy Makers Need Better Information to Protect the Country*, March 2009, http://www.markle.org/ downloadable_assets/20090304_mtf_report.pdf; CSIS Commission on Cybersecurity for the 44th Presidency, *Cybersecurity Two Years Later*, January 2011, http://csis.org/files/publication/ 110128_Lewis_CybersecurityTwoYearsLater_Web.pdf.

[43] See, for example, Greg Nojeim, "WH Cybersecurity Proposal: Questioning the DHS Collection Center," *Center for Democracy & Technology*, May 24, 2011, http://cdt.org/blogs/greg-nojeim/wh-cybersecurity-proposal-questioning-dhs-collection-center; and Adriane Lapointe, *Oversight for Cybersecurity Activities* (Center for Strategic and International Studies, December 7, 2010), http://csis.org/files/publication/101202_Oversight_for_Cybersecurity_Activities.pdf. See also comments received by a Department of Commerce task force (available at http://www.nist.gov/itl/ cybersecnoi.cfm) in conjunction with development of this report: Internet Policy Task Force, *Cybersecurity, Innovation, and the Internet Economy* (Department of Commerce, June 2011), http://www.nist.gov/itl/upload/ Cybersecurity_Green-Paper_FinalVersion.pdf. See also footnote 19.

[44] House Committee on Homeland Security, Subcommittee on Cybersecurity, Infrastructure Protection, and Security Technologies, "Hearing on Draft Legislative Proposal on Cybersecurity," 2011, http://homeland house.gov/hearing/ subcommittee-hearing-hearing-draft-legislative-proposal-cybersecurity.

[45] Department of Homeland Security, "National Cybersecurity and Communications Integration Center", December 6, 2011, http://www.dhs.gov/files/programs/nccic.shtm.

[46] Department of Homeland Security Office of Inspector General, "Secretary Napolitano Opens New National Cybersecurity and Communications Integration Center," Press Release, October 30, 2009, http://www.dhs.gov/ynews/ releases/pr_1256914923094.shtm. The subcommittee version of H.R. 3476 would also have provided statutory (continued...)

3342 would not authorize any new entities but list a set of existing centers to which their information-sharing provisions would apply. The DHS center that the *White House Proposal* would establish (see "DHS Authorities for Protection of Federal Systems") would have information sharing as one of its responsibilities.

- *Establish provisions for sharing classified information.* The *Task Force Report*, H.R. 3523, S. 2105, S. 2151, and S. 3342 would establish procedures to permit sharing of classified cybersecurity information with private-sector entities that meet specific criteria.

- *Establish authority for information sharing by and with private-sector entities.*

  - H.R. 3523 would permit cybersecurity providers or self-protected entities to share threat information with other designated entities, notwithstanding any other provision of law. Federal agencies receiving such information would be required to share it with NCCIC, which could share it with other federal entities upon request of the provider of the information.

  - S. 2105 would expressly permit disclosure of lawfully obtained threat indicators among private-sector entities, with the exchanges the bill would establish, and by federal entities with other relevant federal or private entities, notwithstanding any other provision of law.

  - S. 2151 and S. 3342 would permit nonfederal entities to share threat information with cybersecurity centers or with other nonfederal entities for the purpose of addressing threats. S. 2151 would require providers of communications, remote computing, and cybersecurity services under federal contracts to share with cybersecurity centers, through the contracting agency, any threat information related to the contract. S. 3342 would instead require a coordinated process through which providers would inform federal entities of significant incidents with impacts on their missions, with the entity reporting the information to a cybersecurity center. S. 2151 would permit centers to disclose threat information for specified purposes to federal entities, service providers, and nonfederal government entities, whereas S. 3342 would not permit centers to disclose such information to service providers.

  - The *White House Proposal* would permit nonfederal entities to disclose information to a designated cybersecurity center for purposes of protection from cybersecurity threats and would permit federal agencies to disclose such information to relevant private entities.

- *Limit disclosure of shared information.* The *Task Force Report*, the subcommittee version of H.R. 3674, H.R. 3523, S. 2105, S. 2151, S. 3342, and the *White House Proposal* would all provide exemptions from the "Freedom of Information Act (FOIA)" for cybersecurity information.[47] All would also restrict disclosure in other ways, such as expressly requiring that it be for specified cybersecurity purposes, although specific requirements vary.

(...continued)

authority for NCCIC, but would have given it somewhat different responsibilities.

[47] The committee version of H.R. 3674 includes a FOIA exemption by reference to the amendments to Title XI of the "National Security Act of 1947" that would be made by H.R. 3523.

- *Limit government use of information to specified purposes.* The *Task Force Report*, H.R. 3523, H.R. 3674, S. 2151, and S. 3342 would expressly restrict or prohibit regulatory use of shared information. S. 2105 and the *White House Proposal* would limit use of acquired information to cybersecurity or law enforcement purposes. In addition to those uses, H.R. 3523, S. 2151, and S. 3342 would permit use for national security, and H.R. 3523 would add protection from physical harm and, for minors, from pornography or other sexual exploitation.

- *Limit liability for information sharing.* The *Task Force Report*, H.R. 3523, S. 2105, S. 2151, S. 3342, and the *White House Proposal* would protect nonfederal entities from liability for information shared or other specified actions taken in accordance with the provisions in the legislative proposal. H.R. 3523 would also provide for limited liability for federal violations of restrictions in the bill on disclosure, use, and protection of shared information. The subcommittee version of H.R. 3674 would have permitted actual and punitive civil damages against persons who disclose or use for purposes other than cybersecurity the information that is disclosed to private entities.

- *Provide privacy and civil liberties protections.* All five proposals call for privacy protections. The *Task Force Report* recommends that in providing safe harbors for entities involved in information sharing, "the protection of personal privacy should be at the forefront" (p. 7). It also recommends that the proposed nongovernmental clearinghouse have a privacy board.

  - H.R. 3523 would permit the federal government to "undertake reasonable efforts to limit the impact on privacy and civil liberties" of shared information and require the Inspector General of the Intelligence Community to include, in an annual report to Congress, metrics on impacts of sharing on privacy and civil liberties.[48] It would also require "appropriate" anonymization of shared information.[49] In addition, the bill would prohibit federal use of identifying information from specified sets of library, sales, tax, education, or medical records.

  - The subcommittee version of H.R. 3674 would require that two members of the NISO board of directors be representatives from the privacy and civil liberties community (the committee version), that the NISO charter and procedures include privacy and civil liberties protections, and that anonymization procedures, such as removal of personally identifiable information, be used for shared information. The committee version would create a similar board for the NCCIC and would require ongoing review by the DHS privacy officer of departmental policies and activities.

  - S. 2105 would require the director of the DHS center to appoint a privacy officer, create guidelines for protection of privacy and civil liberties, and ensure that center activities comply with federal requirements. The bill would also require the Secretary of Homeland Security to develop policies and procedures to minimize the impacts of information sharing involving the exchanges that would be established by the bill. It would require three

---

[48] Sec. 1104(c)(7) of the National Security Act as added by Sec. 2(a) of the bill.

[49] Sec. 1104(b)(3)(A) as added.

relevant reports: (1) an annual joint report to Congress by the DHS and Department of Justice privacy officers assessing impacts, (2) a report from the Privacy and Civil Liberties Oversight Board[50] assessing impacts and recommending statutory changes; and (3) a joint report by the Secretary of Homeland Security, the Director of National Intelligence, the Attorney General, and the Secretary of Defense that would include disclosure of significant noncompliance by nonfederal entities with the requirements of the information sharing title of the bill, especially with respect to privacy and civil liberties, with recommendations for any statutory changes.

- S. 2151 would require the heads of agencies with cybersecurity centers to jointly develop procedures for sharing information. Those would consider the need for protection of privacy and civil liberties through anonymization and other means. S. 3342 would in addition permit efforts to limit impacts from sharing on privacy and civil liberties. Both bills would also require biennial joint implementation reports from the agency heads, including review of how shared information may impact privacy and civil liberties, the adequacy of steps to reduce such impact, and any recommended changes to authorities.

- The *White House Proposal* would require that "reasonable efforts" be taken "to remove information that can be used to identify specific persons unrelated to the cybersecurity threat."[51] It would add a new Sec. 248 to the HSA on privacy and civil liberties relating to cybersecurity. It would require the Secretary of Homeland Security, in consultation with privacy and civil liberties experts, to develop and periodically review policies and procedures on information access, disclosure, and use. The policies and procedures would be required to minimize impacts on privacy and civil liberties, safeguard identities, protect confidentiality as much as possible, and provide limits on access, use, and disclosure of information. Agency heads would be required to develop policies for handling information associated with specific persons, to establish programs to monitor and oversee compliance with DHS and agency policies, and to develop and enforce sanctions for violations by agency personnel. The above policies and procedures would be subject to review and approval by the Attorney General. Like S. 2105, the *White House Proposal* would require an annual joint report to Congress by the DHS and Department of Justice privacy officers assessing impacts, and a report from the Privacy and Civil Liberties Oversight Board assessing impacts and recommending statutory changes.

Other Topics

Cybercrime Law. S. 2151, S. 3342, the *White House Proposal,* and the *Task Force Report* would each revise current criminal statutes relating to cybersecurity, including criminalizing the damaging of computers associated with critical infrastructure (CI).[52]

---

[50] The board was established by the "Intelligence Reform and Terrorism Prevention Act of 2004 (IRTPA)."

[51] Sec. 245(a)(1) as added to the HSA by the proposal.

[52] For discussion of federal cybercrime laws, see CRS Report 97-1025, *Cybercrime: An Overview of the Federal Computer Fraud and Abuse Statute and Related Federal Criminal Laws*, by Charles Doyle; and CRS Report R40599, *Identity Theft: Trends and Issues*, by Kristin M. Finklea. See also the discussions of criminal statutes in this report.

Data Breach Notification. The *White House Proposal* and the *Task Force Report* would also both set federal requirements for data breach notification—public notification in cases where a security breach poses significant risks of exposure of sensitive personal information. For more information on this issue, including discussion of bills that would address it, see CRS Report R42474, *Selected Federal Data Security Breach Legislation*, by Kathleen Ann Ruane and CRS Report R42475, *Data Security Breach Notification Laws*, by Gina Stevens.

Some proposals address additional topics not discussed in this overview. For example, H.R. 2096 would require NIST to develop a strategy for federal use of cloud computing. The *White House Proposal* would restrict the power of state and local governments to require business entities to locate data centers within the state or locality. To the extent that such topics are addressed by amending current statutes, they are discussed below under the relevant laws.

Discussion of Proposed Revisions of Current Statutes

To identify laws that might be considered candidates for revision, CRS conducted a broad search, consulting with various experts and examining various sources, including legislative proposals in the 111th and 112th Congresses. That search yielded more than 50 potentially relevant statutes (see **Table 2**), of which proposed revisions were identified for 31.[53] For each of the latter group, the report contains an entry that includes

- the popular name of the statute;[54]

- the public law number, along with Statutes-at-Large and relevant U.S. Code citations;[55]

- a brief description of the relevance of the statute for cybersecurity;[56] and

- discussion of potential revisions or updates that have been suggested.[57]

---

[53] There are 27 entries, but the one on antitrust laws consists of four different statutes. Neither of the two lists is intended to be definitive or exhaustive. For example, some analysts may argue that more agency authorization statutes should be included, or, alternatively, that some of the statutes that are included are not of significant relevance.

[54] This is the name by which the statute is commonly known.

[55] The public law (P.L.) and *United States Statutes at Large* (Stat.) citations refer to the original law to which the popular name currently applies. Laws enacted before 1957 generally do not have public law numbers but chapter numbers (Ch.) instead. U.S. Code (U.S.C.) citations refer to the codified law, including any amendments, of those provisions deemed most relevant for cybersecurity as discussed in the text under that law (see also footnote 56). For more information about citation forms, see Law Library of Congress, "Federal Statutes," April 4, 2011, http://www.loc.gov/law/help/statutes.php. More complete cross-references of public laws to corresponding provisions of U.S. Code can be found in classification tables (see, for example, U.S. House of Representatives, Office of the Law Revision Counsel, "U.S. Code Classification Tables," 2011, http://uscode.house.gov/classification/tables.shtml).

[56] In some cases, such as the Cybersecurity Research And Development Act, P.L. 107-305, the entire statute is relevant to cybersecurity. In others, such as the Omnibus Crime Control and Safe Streets Act of 1968, P.L. 90-351, the statute has a broader focus and only the provisions relevant to the text are cited and described. However, given that cybersecurity is not a precise concept, there may in some cases be legitimate disagreements among experts about which provisions are relevant. Therefore, the descriptions and U.S. Code citations cannot be considered definitive.

[57] The discussion is provided for purposes of information only. CRS does not propose legislation or take positions or make recommendations on legislative proposals or issues. Contributing CRS staff include Patricia Moloney Figliola, Kristin M. Finklea, Eric A. Fischer, Wendy R. Ginsberg, John Rollins, Kathleen Ann Ruane, Gina Stevens, Rita Tehan, (continued...)

Entries are in chronological order.[58] The statutes discussed include only those for which CRS identified specific proposals to revise them from various observers and in public sources.[59] It does not include proposals for new provisions of federal law that were not identified explicitly as revisions of current named statutes.

One example is the recommendations for statutory language on data-breach notification in the *White House Proposal* and the *Task Force Report*. Neither those two documents, nor the bills on the issue that have been introduced in the 112th Congress,[60] specify named statutes to be revised. One of those bills, S. 1151, would revise 18 U.S.C. Chapter 47 (Fraud and False Statements) by adding a new section at the end, but that provision does not modify any named statute specified either in the bill or in the U.S. Code. It is therefore not included in the discussion below. However, the bill would also revise 18 U.S.C. §1030, which was added by the "Counterfeit Access Device and Computer Fraud and Abuse Act of 1984," so that provision is discussed.

Another example is bills with provisions clearly related to a named statute, but that do not explicitly modify that statute. One example from the 111th Congress is H.R. 5590, which had cybersecurity provisions that might be interpreted as modifications to the HSA but were not cited as such. Such provisions are not discussed in this report because their effects on specific statutes could not be determined with certainty.

The approach taken in this report of focusing on statutes by their popular names is useful in many cases, but it has some significant limitations, particularly with respect to the U.S. Code. Some laws, such as the USA Patriot Act of 2001 (see **Table 2**), may be classified across many titles and sections,[61] which may make analysis more challenging. Fortunately, that did not prove to be a significant concern for this report.

However, lack of correspondence between named laws and proposed modification of provisions in the U.S. Code, described above, may in some cases result in significant gaps in coverage of relevant provisions of law relating to cybersecurity by an approach such as the one taken here. Therefore, the analysis presented here should not be regarded as complete.

(...continued)

and Catherine A. Theohary. Entries for which no contributor is indicated were written by Eric A. Fischer.

[58] The order is by date of enactment of the earliest relevant statute, as assessed by CRS. This organization, rather than alternatives such as by topic or U.S. Code title, was chosen because it provides the best view of the evolution of legislation in this area.

[59] Sources are cited where they could be specifically identified.

[60] Data-breach notification is also covered by H.R. 1528, H.R. 1707, H.R. 1841, H.R. 2577, S. 1151, S. 1207, S. 1480, and S. 1535.

[61] This act was classified to 15 titles.

Posse Comitatus Act of 1879

Ch. 263, 20 Stat. 152.
18 U.S.C. §1385.[62]

Major Relevant Provisions

- Restricts the use of military forces in civilian law enforcement within the United States, unless it is within a federal government facility.[63]

- Courts have ruled that violations of the act occur when civilian law enforcement makes "direct active use" of military investigators, when use of the military pervades the activities of the civilian officials, or when the military is used so as to subject citizens to military power that is regulatory, prescriptive, or compulsory in nature.

Possible Updates

- Some observers claim that the act prevents the military from cooperating on cybersecurity with civil agencies that may lack the resident expertise and capabilities of the military and DOD.[64] In addition, it may sometimes be difficult to distinguish a criminal cyber attack from one involving national defense, especially if the attack is on a component of critical infrastructure.

- Some have therefore proposed that the act be amended to clarify when U.S. military can operate domestically regarding cyber threats to such infrastructure, most of which is privately owned. Others maintain that no revision is needed because the President has the authority under current law to direct the military to support civil authorities in the event of a domestic disaster.

- A memorandum of agreement signed between DHS and DOD may increase the likelihood that the military would play a significant role in responding to a major cyber attack on U.S. information networks.[65] However, some argue that the defense of U.S. information systems should be solely the purview of civilian agencies such as DHS and the FBI, because involvement of the military creates unacceptable privacy and civil liberties concerns.

---

[62] Prepared by Catherine A. Theohary, Analyst in National Security Policy and Information Operations (ctheohary@crs.loc.gov, 7-0844).

[63] For further discussion, see CRS Report RS22266, *The Use of Federal Troops for Disaster Assistance: Legal Issues*, by Jennifer K. Elsea and R. Chuck Mason.

[64] For example, see Jeffrey K. Toomer, "A Strategic View of Homeland Security: Relooking the Posse Comitatus Act and DOD's Role in Homeland Security" (monograph, School of Advanced Military Studies, United States Army Command and General Staff College, Fort Leavenworth, Kansas, July 11, 2002), http://www.dtic mil/cgi-bin/GetTRDoc?Location=U2&doc=GetTRDoc.pdf&AD=ADA403866.

[65] Department of Homeland Security and Department of Defense, "Regarding Cybersecurity." The MOA provides terms for sharing of personnel, equipment, and facilities by the two agencies to improve planning, capabilities, and mission activities in national cybersecurity efforts.

Antitrust Laws and Section 5 of the Federal Trade Commission Act

Sherman Antitrust Act

Ch. 647, 26 Stat. 209.
15 U.S.C. §§1-7.

Wilson Tariff Act

Ch. 349, §73, 28 Stat. 570.
15 U.S.C. §§8-11.

Clayton Act

P.L. 63-212, 38 Stat. 730.
15 U.S.C. §§12-27.

Section 5 of the Federal Trade Commission Act (FTC Act)

Ch. 311, §5, 38 Stat. 719.
15 U.S.C. §45(a).[66]

When referred to in statute, the term "antitrust laws" generally means the three laws listed in 15 U.S.C. §12(a), which are the first three statutes listed above. Also frequently included in the list of antitrust laws is Section 5 of the FTC Act, which prohibits unfair and deceptive trade practices. Section 5 is included because courts have found that unfair competition includes, at the least, activity that would violate the Sherman or Clayton Acts.[67]

Major Relevant Provisions

- The antitrust laws as well as Section 5 of the FTC Act are a collection of statutes that forbid combinations or agreements that unreasonably restrain trade.[68] Whenever competitors in a given market share information, antitrust concerns may be raised due to the risk of collusion among competitors.[69]

Possible Updates

Information sharing agreements between private corporations may be subject to antitrust scrutiny, because the sharing of information among competitors could create opportunities for collaboration with the goal of restraining trade.[70] However, information sharing agreements to

---

[66] Prepared by Kathleen Ann Ruane, Legislative Attorney (kruane@crs.loc.gov, 7-9135).

[67] See, e.g., United States v. American Airlines Inc., 743 F.2d 1114 (5th Cir. 1984); FTC v. Motion Picture Advertising Serv. Co., 344 U.S. 392, 394-95 (1953); FTC v. Cement Institute, 333 U.S. 683, 694 (1948); Fashion Originators' Guild v. FTC, 312 U.S. 457, 463-64 (1941).

[68] See Standard Oil Co. v. U.S., 221 U.S. 1 (1911).

[69] See Federal Trade Commission and Department of Justice, *Antitrust Guidelines for Collaborations among Competitors*, April 2000, http://www.ftc.gov/os/2000/04/ftcdojguidelines.pdf.

[70] Ibid.

---

combat cybersecurity may be in compliance with antitrust principles so long as their goals are to combat cyber threats rather than restrain competition.[71]

Some may argue that in order to develop effective and efficient information sharing agreements to combat cybersecurity threats, an explicit exemption from the antitrust laws for these agreements is necessary. Congress has previously proposed such an exemption. For example, H.R. 2435 (107th Congress) would have granted an express exemption from the antitrust laws and from Section 5 of the FTC Act to persons making and implementing agreements entered into solely for the purpose of "facilitating the correction or avoidance of a cyber security-related problem or communication of or disclosing information to help correct or avoid the effects of a cyber security-related problem." Such an exemption, if enacted by Congress, would allow market participants to engage in information sharing for the purposes of combating cybersecurity threats without concern for implicating the antitrust laws. In the 112th Congress, the *Task Force Report* states that an antitrust exemption *might* be required.[72] H.R. 3523 does not specifically mention antitrust laws, but it permits sharing of cybersecurity information among private-sector entities "notwithstanding any other provision of law." S. 2151 and S. 3342 would expressly exempt from antitrust laws the exchange among private entities of information relating to cybersecurity threats.

Others may argue that the antitrust laws are flexible in nature, particularly as they relate to information sharing agreements, and the laws are flexibly applied by the agencies of jurisdiction.[73] This flexible nature may obviate the need for express exemptions from the application of the laws, while keeping the antitrust agencies involved in and aware of the information sharing agreements companies are making.[74] The agencies have expressed a view that if competitors are collaborating for reasons that do not restrain trade or hamper competition, and safeguards are in place to prevent such restraint, the antitrust laws should not hinder such collaboration.[75] The Department of Justice (DOJ) currently allows companies wishing to create information sharing arrangements for permissible and procompetitive purposes to submit their plans for collaboration to the agency.[76] The agency then reviews the plans and, if the plans are approved, issues what is known as a business review letter.[77] The business review letter will generally state that DOJ does not intend to enforce the antitrust laws against the proposed collaboration. DOJ has issued business review letters to companies who have developed plans to share information to combat cybersecurity threats.[78]

---

[71] Ibid. (noting that many collaborations among competitors are "not only benign, but procompetitive").

[72] House Republican Cybersecurity Task Force, *Recommendations*, p. 11.

[73] See Amitai Aviram, "Network Responses to Network Threats," in *The Law and Economics of Cybersecurity*, ed. Mark Grady and Francesco Parisi (New York: Cambridge University Press, 2006), 157-158.

[74] See Federal Trade Commission and Department of Justice, *Antitrust Guidelines*.

[75] Ibid.

[76] 28 C.F.R. §50.6.

[77] Federal Trade Commission and Department of Justice, *Antitrust Guidelines*.

[78] Joel I. Klein, Assistant Attorney General, to Barbara Greenspan, Associate General Counsel, Electric Power Institute, Inc., October 2, 2000, http://www.justice.gov/atr/public/busreview/6614 htm.

National Institute of Standards and Technology Act

Ch. 872, 31 Stat. 1449.
15 U.S.C. §271 et seq.

Major Relevant Provisions

The original act gave the agency responsibilities relating to technical standards. Later amendments added more generally relevant provisions and, more specifically,

- Identified relevant research topics, among them computer and telecommunication systems, including information security and control systems.[79]

- Established a computer standards program at the National Institute of Standards and Technology (NIST).[80]

Possible Updates

Despite NIST's current authority to conduct research on computers and information security, some concerns have been raised about whether those activities should be enhanced in light of the evolving threat environment for cybersecurity. In the 111th Congress, H.R. 4061, which was passed by the House, would have required NIST to conduct intramural research on identity management and the security of information systems, networks, and industrial control systems. A similar bill, H.R. 2096, is being considered by the 112th Congress.

Federal Power Act

Ch. 285, 41 Stat. 1063.
16 U.S.C. §791a et seq., §824 et seq.[81]

Major Relevant Provisions

- Established the Federal Energy Regulatory Commission (FERC) and gave it regulatory authority over interstate sale and transmission of electric power.

Possible Updates

Concerns about the vulnerability of the electric grid to cyber attack have increased substantially over the last several years.[82] Although the Energy Policy Act of 2005 (P.L. 109-58) gave FERC

---

[79] 15 U.S.C. §272, as amended by the Technology Competitiveness Act, Subtitle B of Title V of P.L. 100-418, the Omnibus Trade and Competitiveness Act of 1988, which also changed the name of the agency from the National Bureau of Standards to the National Institute of Standards and Technology, and changed the name of the act to the National Institute of Standards and Technology Act.

[80] 15 U.S.C. §§278g-3 and -4, as added by the Computer Security Act of 1987. See also "Federal Information Security Management Act of 2002 (FISMA)."

[81] The law was originally enacted in 1920 as the Federal Water Power Act but was renamed the Federal Power Act in 1935 (49 Stat. 863, 16 U.S.C. §791a).

[82] See, for example, H.Rept. 111-493, S.Rept. 111-331.

responsibility for developing reliability standards for power systems, limitations to that authority and to the usefulness of the standards-development process to respond effectively to rapidly emerging cybersecurity threats have raised concerns about the need for enhancing FERC's authority to address those threats, especially in light of the development of smart-grid technology.[83] Several bills were introduced in the 111th Congress (H.R. 2165, H.R. 2195, H.R. 5026, S. 946, S. 1462) in response. H.R. 5026, which was passed by the House, would have expanded FERC's jurisdiction over electric infrastructure and authorized FERC to order actions by relevant entities in response to threats to cybersecurity. In the 112th Congress, S. 1342 would also provide expanded cybersecurity authorities to FERC, and H.R. 668 would give FERC emergency authorities in response to events causing large-scale disruptions of the electric grid.

Communications Act of 1934

Ch. 652, 48 Stat. 1064.
47 U.S.C. §151 et seq.[84]

Major Relevant Provisions

- Established the Federal Communications Commission (FCC) and gave it regulatory authority over both domestic and international commercial wired and wireless communications.

- Provides the President with authority in a national emergency to control "any or all stations or devices capable of emitting electromagnetic radiations," and in case of war or threat of war, to close "any facility or station for wire communication" (Sec. 706 of the act, 47 U.S.C. §606).

Possible Updates

Some observers have proposed that the act should be revised to give the FCC more of a role in cybersecurity, especially given the growing merging of information and communications technology (ICT) and their increasing importance in the U.S. economy. In fact, a number of other countries have more unified governance of ICT than the United States.[85]

Some controversy exists about whether the Section 706 authorities described above permit the President to shut down Internet communications during a war or national emergency, a power that has sometimes been referred to as the "Internet kill switch."[86] However, there does not appear to be a consensus about whether in fact such additional authority is needed, or, if it is not, whether additional legislation is needed to clarify and delimit it.

That debate became acute during Senate consideration of S. 773 and S. 3480 in the 111th Congress. Those bills would have authorized emergency measures by the President if the

---

[83] CRS Report R41886, *The Smart Grid and Cybersecurity—Regulatory Policy and Issues*, by Richard J. Campbell.

[84] See also "Communications Decency Act of 1996."

[85] See, for example, Elgin M. Brunner and Manuel Suter, *International CIIP Handbook 2008/2009* (Center for Security Studies, ETH Zurich, 2008), http://www.css.ethz.ch/publications/CIIP_HB_08.

[86] See also CRS Report R41674, *Terrorist Use of the Internet: Information Operations in Cyberspace*, by Catherine A. Theohary and John Rollins.

operation of critical infrastructure were threatened by cyber attack. A similar provision has been proposed in S. 413 in the 112th Congress.[87] This bill also contains a provision that would expressly deny the federal government of any authority to "shut down the Internet."

National Security Act of 1947

Ch. 343, 61 Stat. 495
50 U.S.C. 401 et seq.

Major Relevant Provisions

- Provided the basis for the modern organization of U.S. defense and national security by reorganizing military and intelligence functions in the federal government.

- Created the National Security Council, the Central Intelligence Agency, and the position of Secretary of Defense.

- Established procedures for access to classified information.

Possible Updates

A broad consensus exists that a significant barrier to improving cybersecurity is limitations on sharing of information, including classified information, about cyber-threats and attacks.[88] H.R. 3523 would address that concern by amending the act to facilitate sharing of intelligence information relating to cybersecurity, including classified information, between federal intelligence entities and private-sector providers of cybersecurity services, and to facilitate the identification and sharing of threat information by providers. The bill also includes provisions for protection from liability for entities sharing information and exemption from disclosure of that information under the "Freedom of Information Act (FOIA)."

See also "Information Sharing."

---

[87] S. 413 is largely identical to S. 3480. Both would provide the authority for the emergency measures through a revision of the Homeland Security Act, not the Communications Act. In addition, they would assign the authority to implement Sec. 706 to the head of a White House office to be created by the bills. The provision in S. 773 was not presented as a revision to a specified law.

[88] For example, the *Task Force Report* states, "There is widespread agreement that greater sharing of information is needed within industries, among industries, and between government and industry in order to improve cybersecurity and to prevent and respond to rapidly changing threats. For example, through intelligence collection, the federal government has insights and capabilities that many times are classified but would be useful to help defend private companies from cybersecurity attacks" (House Republican Cybersecurity Task Force, *Recommendations*, p. 10).

U.S. Information and Educational Exchange Act of 1948 (Smith-Mundt Act)

Ch. 36, 62 Stat. 6.
22 U.S.C. §1431 et seq.[89]

Major Relevant Provisions

- Restricts the State Department from disseminating public diplomacy information domestically and limits its authority to communicate with the American public in general (22 U.S.C. §1461-1a).[90] The domestic dissemination provision originally applied to the now defunct U.S. Information Agency (USIA), which was abolished and its functions transferred to the Secretary of State by P.L. 105-277 (22 U.S.C. §6532).[91]

Possible Updates

Critics maintain that the law is a Cold War relic intended only to restrict the USIA, which no longer exists, from propagandizing Americans with public diplomacy and information materials that were intended for a foreign audience. Those critics argue that the restrictions were created before the advent of the Internet, and the provisions create an obsolete barrier that serves only to prevent the State Department from communicating effectively. Some have also argued that the law has been interpreted to prohibit the military from conducting information operations in cyberspace, as some of those activities could be considered propaganda that could reach U.S. citizens, since the United States does not restrict Internet access according to territorial boundaries.

Yearly appropriations bills for both the State Department and Department of Defense include restrictions on use of funds for "propaganda" activities, although the word "propaganda" is not defined. In the 111th Congress, H.R. 5729 would have removed the so-called "firewall" between domestic and foreign audiences by explicitly authorizing the Department of State to disseminate information through the Internet and information media, stating that the resolution shall "not be construed to prohibit the Department from engaging in any medium of information on a presumption that a U.S. domestic audience may be exposed to program material." However, this provision would have applied only to the State Department; it would not have included DOD or other federal departments or agencies.

---

[89] Prepared by Catherine A. Theohary, Analyst in National Security Policy and Information Operations (ctheohary@crs.loc.gov, 7-0844).

[90] This restriction was added by the Foreign Relations Authorization Act, Fiscal Years 1986 and 1987 (P.L. 99-93, 99 Stat. 431) and was not part of the original act.

[91] For discussion, see CRS Report R40989, *U.S. Public Diplomacy: Background and Current Issues*, by Kennon H. Nakamura and Matthew C. Weed.

State Department Basic Authorities Act of 1956

Ch. 841, 70 Stat. 890.
22 U.S.C. §2651a.

Major Relevant Provisions

- Specifies the organization of the Department of State, including the positions of coordinator for counterterrorism and for HIV/AIDS response.

Possible Updates

As the Internet becomes increasingly international, concerns have been raised about the development and coordination of international efforts in cybersecurity by the United States.[92] In the 111th Congress, S. 3193 would have addressed those concerns by establishing a coordinator for cyberspace and cybersecurity issues within the Department of State. S. 1426 in the 112th Congress contains a similar provision.

Freedom of Information Act (FOIA)

P.L. 89-487, 80 Stat. 250.
5 U.S.C. §552.[93]

Major Relevant Provisions

- Enables any person to access—without explanation or justification—existing, identifiable, unpublished executive-branch agency records, unless the material falls within any of FOIA's nine categories of exemption from disclosure.

Possible Updates

Sharing of cybersecurity information between the federal government and nonfederal entities is widely considered to be an essential need, especially with respect to the protection of critical infrastructure (CI). However, attempts to encourage the private sector to share sensitive CI information with the federal government have, at times, been met with concerns that such records could be subject to public release under FOIA, resulting in potential economic or other harm to the source.

Among the nine exemptions that permit agencies to withhold applicable records are three that may particularly apply to cybersecurity information:

---

[92] See, for example, CSIS Commission on Cybersecurity for the 44th Presidency, *Securing Cyberspace for the 44th Presidency*, December 2008, http://www.csis.org/tech/cyber/; The White House, *Cyberspace Policy Review*, May 29, 2009, http://www.whitehouse.gov/assets/documents/Cyberspace_Policy_Review_final.pdf; and The White House, *International Strategy for Cyberspace*.

[93] Prepared by Wendy R. Ginsberg, Analyst in Government Organization and Management (wginsberg@crs.loc.gov, 7-3933).

- *Exemption 1:* information properly classified for national defense or foreign policy purposes as secret under criteria established by an executive order.

- *Exemption 3:* data specifically exempted from disclosure by a statute other than FOIA if that statute meets criteria laid out in FOIA.[94]

- *Exemption 4:* trade secrets and commercial or financial information obtained from a person that is privileged or confidential.[95]

An example of Exemption 3 is Sec. 214 of the HSA (see p. 40), which exempts information about the security of critical infrastructure and protected systems that is voluntarily submitted to an agency covered under the act, provided that the entity that supplies the information expressly requests the exemption concurrently.

Despite these existing protections, some private-sector entities may still have concerns about public release of sensitive records—that existing laws may not be specific enough to protect particular types of records, or they may be too narrow to protect all records of concern. The *White House Proposal* would address such concerns by applying Exemption 3 to any lawfully obtained information provided to DHS for cybersecurity purposes.[96] The *Task Force Report* also suggests that a FOIA exemption may be needed,[97] and several bills, including H.R. 3523, S. 2105, S. 2151, and S. 3342http://www.congress.gov/cgi-lis/bdquery/z?d112:S.2151:, would provide such a FOIA exemption, although none of those proposals would directly modify the statute. Adding such broad exemptions to FOIA, however, could nevertheless prompt concerns about decreases in federal transparency.

---

[94] The statute must require that the data be withheld from the public in such a manner as to leave no discretion on the issue, establish particular criteria for withholding information or refer to particular types of matters to be withheld, or specifically cite the exemption if enacted after October 28, 2009, the date of enactment of the OPEN FOIA Act of 2009, P.L. 111-83. These exemptions are also called "b(3) exemptions" because they are created pursuant to 5 U.S.C. §552(b)(3).

[95] Other exemptions may also sometimes apply to cybersecurity information. For further discussion of FOIA and its exemptions, see CRS Report R41933, *Freedom of Information Act (FOIA): Background and Policy Options for the 112th Congress*, by Wendy Ginsberg, CRS Report R41406, *The Freedom of Information Act and Nondisclosure Provisions in Other Federal Laws* , by Gina Stevens.

[96] See "Sec. 245. Voluntary Disclosure of Cybersecurity Information," in The White House, "Department of Homeland Security Cybersecurity Authority and Information Sharing," May 12, 2011, p. 8–9, http://www.whitehouse.gov/sites/default/files/omb/legislative/letters/dhs-cybersecurity-authority.pdf.

[97] Specifically, it states, "information sharing within existing structures can be improved through limited safe harbors when private sector entities voluntarily disclose threat, vulnerability, or incident information to the federal government or ask for advice or assistance to help increase protections on their own systems. These protections would need to address concerns about antitrust issues, liability, an exemption from the Freedom of Information Act (FOIA), protection from public disclosure, protection from regulatory use by government, and whether or not a private entity is operating as an agent of the government. However, the protection of personal privacy should be at the forefront of any limited legal protection proposal" (House Republican Cybersecurity Task Force, *Recommendations*, p. 11).

Omnibus Crime Control and Safe Streets Act of 1968

P.L. 90-351, 82 Stat. 197.
42 USC Chapter 46, §§3701 to 3797ee-1.

Major Relevant Provisions

- Title I established federal grant programs and other forms of assistance to state and local law enforcement.

- Title III is a comprehensive wiretapping and electronic eavesdropping statute that not only outlawed both activities in general terms but that also permitted federal and state law enforcement officers to use them under strict limitations.[98]

Possible Updates

The incidence of cybercrime has increased dramatically over the last decade.[99] State and local law enforcement agencies play an important role in combating cybercrime, but concerns have been raised about their abilities to invest sufficient resources in enforcement activities. In the 111th Congress, H.R. 1292 would have added a program for law enforcement grants to state and local criminal justice agencies and relevant nonprofit organizations to combat "white collar crime," including cybercrime.

Racketeer Influenced and Corrupt Organizations Act (RICO)

P.L. 91-452, 84 Stat. 941.
18 U.S.C. Chapter 96, §§1961-1968.

Major Relevant Provisions

- Enlarges the civil and criminal consequences of a list of state and federal crimes when committed in a way characteristic of the conduct of organized crime (racketeering).[100]

Possible Updates

The *Task Force Report* recommends that Congress change RICO "to include computer fraud within the definition of racketeering." [101] The *White House Proposal* would make felony violation

---

[98] These provisions, along with possible updates, are discussed under "Electronic Communications Privacy Act of 1986."

[99] There is no uniform definition of "cybercrime." Furthermore, no definitive statistics on cybercrime appear to be publically available. However, the public/private Internet Crime Complaint Center referred 25 times as many of the complaints it received to law enforcement agencies in 2010 (121,710) as in 2001 (4,810) (Internet Crime Complaint Center, *2010 Internet Crime Report*, 2011, http://www.ic3.gov/media/annualreport/2010_IC3Report.pdf).

[100] For details, CRS Report 96-950, *RICO: A Brief Sketch*, by Charles Doyle.

[101] House Republican Cybersecurity Task Force, *Recommendations*, p. 14.

of 18 U.S.C. §1030 (see "Counterfeit Access Device and Computer Fraud and Abuse Act of 1984") a racketeering predicate offense.

Federal Advisory Committee Act (FACA)

P.L. 93-579, 86 Stat 770.
5 U.S.C. App., §§1-16.

Major Relevant Provisions

- Specifies the circumstances under which a federal advisory committee can be established, and its responsibilities and limitations.

- Requires that meetings of such committees be open to the public and that records be available for public inspection.[102]

Possible Updates

The act has been criticized as potentially impeding the full development of public/private partnerships in cybersecurity, particularly with respect to impeding private-sector communications and input on policy.[103] While Sec. 871 of the HSA provides the Secretary of Homeland Security with the power to establish advisory committees that are exempt from the requirements of the act, it is possible that additional exemption authority would be helpful. Any such potential benefits might, however, need to be weighed against the impact of such authority on the public's ability to participate in and access the records of affected advisory committees. The draft bill being considered by the House Committee on Homeland Security[104] would exempt the organization created by the bill from requirements of the act.

Privacy Act of 1974

P.L. 93-579, 88 Stat. 1896.
5 U.S.C. §552a.

Major Relevant Provisions

- Limits the disclosure of personally identifiable information (PII) held by federal agencies.

- Requires agencies to provide access to persons with agency records containing information on them.

---

[102] For more information, see CRS Report R40520, *Federal Advisory Committees: An Overview*, by Wendy Ginsberg.

[103] Isabelle Abele-Wigert and Myriam Dunn, *International CIIP Handbook 2006, Vol. I* (Center for Security Studies, ETH Zurich, 2006), p. 337, http://www.css.ethz.ch/publications/CIIP_HB_06_Vol.1.pdf; Brunner and Suter, *International CIIP Handbook 2008/2009*, p. 456.

[104] House Committee on Homeland Security, "Hearing on Draft Legislative Proposal on Cybersecurity."

- Established a code of fair information practices for collection, management, and dissemination of records by agencies, including requirements for security and confidentiality of records.

Possible Updates

Some observers argue that the act should be revised to clarify, in the context of cybersecurity, what is considered PII and how it can be used, such as by explicitly permitting the sharing among federal agencies—or with appropriate third parties such as owners and operators of critical infrastructure—of certain information, such as a computer's Internet (IP) address, in examinations of threats, vulnerabilities, and attacks. The act contains some exemptions, such as for law enforcement activities (5 U.S.C. §552a(b)(7)) and duties of the Comptroller General (5 U.S.C. §552a(b)(10)), but none relating specifically to cybersecurity. However, other observers may argue that the provisions in the act are sufficient to permit necessary cybersecurity activities, and that revising the act to provide additional authorities relating to cybersecurity could compromise the protections provided by the act. [105] In the 112th Congress, H.R. 1732 would revise the act to take changes in information technology into account, but does not specifically address information relating to cybersecurity.

Counterfeit Access Device and Computer Fraud and Abuse Act of 1984

P.L. 98-473, 98 Stat. 2190.
18 U.S.C. §1030.

Major Relevant Provisions

As amended, [106]

- Provides criminal penalties, including asset forfeiture, for unauthorized access and wrongful use of computers and networks of the federal government or financial institutions, or in interstate or foreign commerce or communication;

- Specifies wrongful use as obtaining protected information, damaging or threatening to damage a computer, using the computer to commit fraud, trafficking in stolen computer passwords, and espionage;

- Criminalized electronic trespassing on and exceeding authorized access to federal government computers; and

- Created a statutory exemption for intelligence and law enforcement activities. [107]

---

[105] For information on how they have been interpreted by the courts, see Department of Justice, "Overview of the Privacy Act of 1974, 2010 Edition," March 2, 2010, http://www.justice.gov/opcl/1974privacyact-overview htm.

[106] The Computer Fraud and Abuse Act of 1986 (P.L. 99-474, 100 Stat. 1213) expanded the scope of the original act. For government computers, it criminalized electronic trespassing, exceeding authorized access, and destroying information. It also criminalized trafficking in stolen computer passwords and created a statutory exemption for intelligence and law enforcement activities.

[107] For more information, see CRS Report 97-1025, *Cybercrime: An Overview of the Federal Computer Fraud and* (continued...)

Possible Update

The *White House Proposal* would add penalties for damaging certain critical infrastructure computers, increase penalties for most violations of the act, clarify certain offenses, and modify the act's conspiracy and forfeiture provisions. In the 112th Congress, S. 2111, S. 2151, and S. 3342 have similar provisions. S. 890, S. 2151, S. 3342, and the White House Proposal would enlarge the scope of the password trafficking offense by removing the requirement that the computer affect interstate commerce or be used by the United States. S. 1151 would also make several changes similar to but not as extensive as those in the Administration proposal.[108] The *Task Force Report* recommends that the act be broadened to cover critical infrastructure systems, and possibly all private-sector computers, with increased criminal penalties. It also recommends that provisions should be focused narrowly enough to avoid creating unintended liability for legitimate activities.[109]

Electronic Communications Privacy Act of 1986 (ECPA)

P.L. 99-508, 100 Stat. 1848.
18 U.S.C. §§2510-2522, 18 U.S.C. §§2701-2712, 18 U.S.C. §§3121-3126.[110]

Major Relevant Provisions

- Attempts to strike a balance between the fundamental privacy rights of citizens and the legitimate needs of law enforcement with respect to data shared or stored in various types of electronic and telecommunications services.[111] Since the act was passed the Internet and associated technologies have expanded exponentially.[112] The act consists of three parts:

(...continued)

Abuse Statute and Related Federal Criminal Laws, by Charles Doyle.

[108] See CRS Report R41941, *The Obama Administration's Cybersecurity Proposal: Criminal Provisions*, by Gina Stevens.

[109] House Republican Cybersecurity Task Force, *Recommendations*, p. 14.

[110] Prepared by Gina Stevens, Legislative Attorney (gstevens@crs.loc.gov, 7-2581).

[111] 100 Stat. 1848; see also House Committee on the Judiciary, "Electronic Communications Privacy Act of 1986," H.Rept. 99-647, 99th Cong. 2d Sess. 2, at 19 (1986).

[112] House Committee on the Judiciary, Subcommittee on the Constitution, Civil Rights, and Civil Liberties, *ECPA Reform and the Revolution in Cloud Computing*, 2010, http://judiciary.house.gov/hearings/hear_100923.html (statement of Edward W. Felton, Professor Princeton University):

> In 1986, when ECPA was passed, the Internet consisted of a few thousand computers. The network was run by the U.S. government for research and education purposes, and commercial activity was forbidden. There were no web pages, because the web had not been invented. Google would not be founded for another decade. Twitter would not be founded for another two decades. Mark Zuckerberg, who would grow up to start Facebook, was two years old. In talking about advances in computing, people often focus on the equipment. Certainly the advances in computing equipment since 1986 have been spectacular. Compared to the high-end supercomputers of 1986, today's mobile phones have more memory, more computing horsepower, and a better network connection not to mention a vastly lower price.

- A revised Title III of the "Omnibus Crime Control and Safe Streets Act of 1968" (also known as "Title III" or the "Wiretap Act")[113] prohibits the interception of wire, oral, or electronic communications unless an exception to the general rule applies. Unless otherwise provided, prohibits wiretapping and electronic eavesdropping; possession of wiretapping or electronic eavesdropping equipment; use or disclosure of information obtained through illegal wiretapping or electronic eavesdropping; and disclosure of information secured through court-ordered wiretapping or electronic eavesdropping, in order to obstruct justice.[114]

- The Stored Communications Act (SCA)[115] prohibits unlawful access to stored communications.[116]

- The Pen Register and Trap and Trace statute governing the installation and use of trap and trace devices and pen registers,[117] proscribing unlawful use of a pen register or a trap and trace device.[118]

- Establishes rules that law enforcement must follow before they can access data stored by service providers. Depending on the type of customer information involved and the type of service being provided, the authorization law enforcement must obtain in order to require disclosure by a third party will range from a simple subpoena to a search warrant based on probable cause.

Possible Updates

ECPA reform efforts focus on crafting a legal structure that is up-to-date, can be effectively applied to modern technology, and that protects users' reasonable expectations of privacy. ECPA is viewed by many stakeholders as unwieldy, complex, and difficult for judges to apply.[119] Cloud computing[120] poses particular challenges to the ECPA framework. For example, when law enforcement officials seek data or files stored in the cloud, such as web-based e-mail applications or online word processing services, the privacy standard that is applied is often lower than the standard that applies when law enforcement officials seek the same data stored on an individual's personal or business hard drive.[121]

---

[113] 18 U.S.C. §2510-2522.

[114] 18 U.S.C. §2511.

[115] 18 U.S.C. §§2701-2712.

[116] 18 U.S.C. §2701.

[117] 18 U.S.C. §§3121-3126. A trap and trace device identifies the source of incoming calls, and a pen register indicates the numbers called from a particular phone.

[118] 18 U.S.C. §3121.

[119] J. Beckwith Burr, "The Electronic Communications Privacy Act of 1986: Principles for Reform," March 30, 2010, http://www.digitaldueprocess.org/files/DDP_Burr_Memo.pdf.

[120] "Cloud computing is an emerging form of computing that relies on Internet-based services and resources to provide computing services to customers, while freeing them from the burden and costs of maintaining the underlying infrastructure. Examples of cloud computing include web-based e-mail applications and common business applications that are accessed online through a browser, instead of through a local computer" (Government Accountability Office, *Information Security: Federal Guidance Needed to Address Control Issues with Implementing Cloud Computing*, GAO-10-513, May 2010, http://www.gao.gov/new.items/d10513.pdf).

[121] House Committee on the Judiciary, Subcommittee on the Constitution, Civil Rights, and Civil Liberties, *ECPA* (continued...)

An ECPA reform advocacy coalition has advanced the following principles:

- A governmental entity may require an entity covered by ECPA (a provider of wire or electronic communication service or a provider of remote computing service) to disclose communications that are not readily accessible to the public, but only with a search warrant issued based on a showing of probable cause, regardless of the age of the communications, the means or status of their storage or the provider's access to or use of the communications in its normal business operations.

- A governmental entity may access, or may require a covered entity to provide, prospectively or retrospectively, location information regarding a mobile communications device, but only with a warrant issued based on a showing of probable cause.

- A governmental entity may access, or may require a covered entity to provide, prospectively or in real time, dialed number information, e-mail to and from information or other data currently covered by the authority for pen registers and trap and trace devices, but only after judicial review and a court finding that the governmental entity has made a showing at least as strong as the showing under 2703(d).

- Where the Stored Communications Act authorizes a subpoena to acquire information, a governmental entity may use such subpoenas only for information related to a specified account(s) or individual(s). All nonparticularized requests must be subject to judicial approval.[122]

The *Task Force Report* recommends changes to laws governing the protection of electronic communications to facilitate sharing of appropriate cybersecurity information, including the development of an anonymous reporting mechanism.[123]

Department of Defense Appropriations Act, 1987

P.L. 99-591, 100 Stat. 3341-82, 3341-122.
10 U.S.C. §167.[124]

Major Relevant Provisions

- Provides specific authority to the U.S. Special Operations Command (USSOCOM) for the conduct of direct action, strategic reconnaissance,

---

(...continued)

Reform and the Revolution in Cloud Computing (statement of Michael Hintze, Associate General Counsel, Microsoft Corp.).

[122] Digital Due Process Coalition, "Our Principles", 2010, http://www.digitaldueprocess.org/index.cfm?objectid=99629E40-2551-11DF-8E02000C296BA163.

[123] House Republican Cybersecurity Task Force, *Recommendations*, p. 14. For more information on ECPA, see CRS Report 98-326, *Privacy: An Overview of Federal Statutes Governing Wiretapping and Electronic Eavesdropping*, by Gina Stevens and Charles Doyle.

[124] Prepared by John Rollins, Specialist in Terrorism and National Security (jrollins@crs.loc.gov, 7-5529).

unconventional warfare, foreign internal defense, civil affairs, and psychological operations; also counterterrorism, humanitarian assistance, theater search and rescue, and such other activities as may be specified by the President or the Secretary of Defense.

Possible Update

In addition to the authority provided under this act, Title 10 of the U.S. Code provides inherent and specific authority to DOD to undertake the following activities:

- §113 provides that, subject to the direction of the President, the Secretary of Defense has authority, direction, and control over DOD;

- §164 provides specific authority for combatant commanders for the performance of missions assigned by the President or by the Secretary with the approval of the President.

Specific authorities for combatant commanders are provided in Title 10 to use force in self-defense and for mission accomplishment—including in the recently recognized information operations environment. In preparing for contingencies or military operations, DOD undertakes activities to lessen risks to U.S. interests, including discrete actions to prepare for and respond to a cyberwarfare-related incident.[125]

Some military activities are conducted *clandestinely* to conceal the nature of the operation and passively collect intelligence. Activities focused on influencing the governing of a foreign country are deemed *covert* actions[126] and may not be conducted by members of the military absent a presidential finding and notification of the congressional intelligence committees.[127]

Some analysts suggest that in the cyber domain distinguishing between whether an action is or should be considered covert or clandestine is problematic, as an attacking adversary's intent and location are often difficult to discern. Should this act be updated, reassessing DOD's authorities in light of its unique intelligence capabilities may assist in responding to and conducting offensive cyber attacks.

High Performance Computing Act of 1991

P.L. 102-194, 105 Stat. 1594.
15 U.S.C. Chapter 81.[128]

---

[125] CRS Report RL31787, *Information Operations, Cyberwarfare, and Cybersecurity: Capabilities and Related Policy Issues*, by Catherine A. Theohary.

[126] 50 U.S.C. §413b(e) defines a covert action as "an activity or activities of the United States Government to influence political, economic, or military conditions abroad, where it is intended that the role of the United States Government will not be apparent or acknowledged publicly, but does not include … activities the primary purpose of which is to acquire intelligence … [or] traditional military activities or routine support to such activities."

[127] For an explanation and analysis of issues relating to covert and clandestine activities see CRS Report RL33715, *Covert Action: Legislative Background and Possible Policy Questions*, by Richard F. Grimmett.

[128] Parts of the chapter have also been given other popular names: the Next Generation Internet Research Act of 1998 (P.L. 105-305), and the Department of Energy High-End Computing Revitalization Act of 2004.

Major Relevant Provisions

- Establishes a federal high-performance computing program and requires that it address security needs.

- Requires that the program provide for interagency coordination and that an annual report on implementation be submitted to Congress.

- Requires NIST to establish security and privacy standards in high-performance computing for federal systems.

Possible Updates

This act established the Networking and Information Technology Research and Development (NITRD) Program, which produces the required annual report. However, concerns have been raised that the program does not yield sufficient strategic planning and does not sufficiently stress cybersecurity research and development (R&D). In the 111th Congress, H.R. 2020, which passed the House, would have addressed that concern by requiring a five-year strategic plan with three-year reviewing cycle. It would also have added a research goal of increasing understanding "of the scientific principles of cyber-physical systems" and improving methods for designing, developing, and operating such systems with high reliability, safety, and security. H.R. 3834 in the 112th Congress is similar but adds provisions on cloud computing. S. 773 in the 111th Congress would have required NIST to develop cybersecurity standards and metrics for computer networks and user interfaces, as would S. 2105 in the 112th Congress. S. 2151 and S. 3342 would establish cybersecurity, including security of supply chains, as one of the goals for research under the act and contains a requirement similar to that of H.R. 3834 for cyber-physical systems. H.R. 3834, S. 2151, and S. 3342 would also make a number of other amendments not directly related to cybersecurity.

Communications Assistance for Law Enforcement Act of 1994 (CALEA)

P.L. 103-414, 108 Stat. 4279.
47 U.S.C. §1001 et seq.[129]

Major Relevant Provisions

- Requires telecommunications carriers to assist law enforcement in performing electronic surveillance on their digital networks pursuant to court orders or other lawful authorization.

- Directs the telecommunications industry to design, develop, and deploy solutions that meet requirements for carriers to support authorized electronic surveillance, including unobtrusive isolation of communications and call-identifying information for a target and provision of that information to law enforcement, in

---

[129] Prepared by Patricia Moloney Figliola, Specialist in Internet and Telecommunications Policy (pfigliola@crs.loc.gov, 7-2508).

a manner that does not compromise the privacy and security of other communications.

Possible Updates

Some government and industry observers believe that CALEA should be revised to improve its effectiveness in addressing cybersecurity concerns. Among the concerns expressed are whether the act is the best mechanism for collecting information transmitted via the Internet, whether reassessment is needed of which private-sector entities the act covers and which government entities should be involved in enforcement and oversight, and what the role of industry should be in the development of the technologies and standards used to implement the provisions of the act. The *Task Force Report* recommends changes to laws governing the protection of electronic communications to facilitate sharing of appropriate cybersecurity information, including the development of an anonymous reporting mechanism.[130]

Communications Decency Act of 1996

P.L. 104-104 (Title V), 110 Stat. 133.
47 U.S.C. §§223, 230.[131]

Major Relevant Provisions

- Intended to regulate indecency and obscenity on telecommunications systems, including the Internet. Although much of the law is targeted at lewd or pornographic material, particularly when shown to children under the age of 18, the obscenity and harassment provisions could also be interpreted as applying to graphic, violent terrorist propaganda or incendiary language.

- Section 230(c)(1) asserts that "no provider or user of an interactive computer service shall be treated as the publisher or speaker of any information." This has been interpreted to absolve Internet service providers and certain web-based services of responsibility for third-party content residing on those networks or websites.[132]

Possible Updates

Some argue that certain Internet content, such as terrorist chat rooms or propaganda websites, presents a national security or operational threat that is not represented within the Communications Decency Act. Further, should such material be deemed as "indecent," the law does not give federal agencies the authority to require that the Internet service providers hosting the content to take it offline.

---

[130] House Republican Cybersecurity Task Force, *Recommendations*, p. 14.

[131] Prepared by Catherine A. Theohary, Analyst in National Security Policy and Information Operations (ctheohary@crs.loc.gov, 7-0844). These provisions are codified to Chapter 5 of Title 47, the "Communications Act of 1934." Codification of the various provisions of this act is complex. See 47 U.S.C. §609 nt. for details.

[132] See CRS Report R41499, *The Communications Decency Act: Section 230(c)(1) and Online Intermediary Liability*, by Kathleen Ann Ruane and Julia Tamulis.

These critics maintain that the law should be revised to compel ISPs and web administrators to dismantle sites containing information that could be used to incite harm against the United States. A possible revision could be similar to the "take down and put back" provision in the Digital Millennium Copyright Act, 112 Stat. 2860, P.L. 105-304 which amended title 17 of the U.S. Code to hold a service liable for publishing material that is defamatory or infringes upon a third party copyright.

Others maintain that such a revision is counter to the spirit of free, open exchange of information that is characterized by the Internet and may be a First Amendment violation. Some have also expressed concerns that the intelligence value gained by preserving and monitoring the sites outweighs the potential threat risk.

Clinger-Cohen Act (Information Technology Management Reform Act) of 1996

P.L. 104-106 (Divisions D and E), 110 Stat. 642.
40 U.S.C. §11101 et seq.[133]

Major Relevant Provisions

- Gave agency heads authority to acquire IT and required them to ensure the adequacy of agency information security policies.

- Established the position of agency Chief Information Officer (CIO), responsible for assisting agency heads in IT acquisition and management.

- Requires the Office of Management and Budget (OMB) to oversee major information technology (IT) acquisitions.

- Requires OMB to promulgate, in consultation with the Secretary of Homeland Security, compulsory federal computer standards based on those developed by the National Institute of Standards and Technology (NIST).[134]

- Exempts national security systems from most provisions.

Possible Update

With the increasing globalization of the IT hardware and software industries, concerns have been growing among cybersecurity experts about potential vulnerabilities at various points along the supply chain for IT products. H.R. 1136, introduced in the 112th Congress, would address such concerns with respect to federal acquisition of IT products and services by requiring vendors to

---

[133] Prepared by Wendy R. Ginsberg, Analyst in Government Organization and Management (wginsberg@crs.loc.gov, 7-3933), and Eric A. Fischer. The two divisions, originally known as the Federal Acquisition Reform Act and the Information Technology Management Reform Act, were renamed as the Clinger-Cohen Act by P.L. 104-208 and reclassified into 40 U.S.C. Subtitle III by P.L. 107-217 (see 40 U.S.C. §101 nt.).

[134] The Clinger-Cohen Act originally gave this promulgation authority to the Secretary of Commerce, while providing the President authority to disapprove or modify such standards, and gave the Secretary authority to waive the standards in specific cases to avoid adverse financial or mission-related impacts. The "Federal Information Security Management Act of 2002 (FISMA)", enacted as part of the Homeland Security Act, transferred that authority to OMB.

meet security requirements to be developed by OMB, and also requiring vulnerability assessments by agencies.

S. 413 (similar to S. 3480 in the 111th Congress), S. 2105, S. 2151, S. 3342, and the *White House Proposal* would return the authority for promulgating standards for federal systems to the Secretary of Commerce.[135] H.R. 4257, in contrast, would not amend that provision.

Congress and the executive branch have debated the limits of the authority and jurisdiction of CIOs since their establishment. In the private sector, CIOs may often serve as the senior IT decision maker. In federal agencies, in contrast, CIOs do not have budgetary control or authority over IT resources.[136] As part of a plan to reform federal IT management,[137] the Obama Administration has indicated its intention to change the role of CIOs "away from just policymaking and infrastructure maintenance, to encompass true portfolio management for all IT," including information security.[138] The *White House Proposal* does not include any provisions related to that proposed change, but additional legislative authority may be required for such a change to be fully implemented.

The Obama Administration also appointed a federal chief information officer and a federal chief technology officer (CTO), positions first created in the George W. Bush Administration, where the OMB deputy director of management also served as federal CIO. In the 111th Congress, H.R. 1910 and H.R. 5136, and H.R. 1136 in the 112th Congress, contain provisions to establish a statutory basis for the CTO position, not, however, explicitly as amendments to the Clinger-Cohen Act.[139] Some proposals in previous Congresses would also have established the federal CIO position in law.[140]

Identity Theft and Assumption Deterrence Act of 1998

P.L. 105-318, 112 Stat. 3007.
18 U.S.C. §1028.[141]

---

[135] See the discussion of FISMA, p. 42.

[136] They do have authority under FISMA to ensure compliance with that law's information security requirements (44 U.S.C. §3544). Some agency CIOs also have statutory authority in addition to that provided by Clinger-Cohen and FISMA. For example, the CIO of the intelligence community has procurement approval authority for IT (50 U.S.C. §403-3g), and CIOs within DOD have budgetary review authority (10 U.S.C. §2223).

[137] Vivek Kundra, *25-Point Implementation Plan to Reform Federal Information Technology Management* (The White House, December 9, 2010), http://www.cio.gov/documents/25-Point-Implementation-Plan-to-Reform-Federal%20IT.pdf.

[138] Jacob J. Lew, "Chief Information Officer Authorities," Memorandum for the Heads of Executive Departments and Agencies, M-11-29, August 8, 2011, pp. 1–2, http://www.whitehouse.gov/sites/default/files/omb/memoranda/2011/m11-29.pdf.

[139] See CRS Report R40150, *A Federal Chief Technology Officer in the Obama Administration: Options and Issues for Consideration*, by John F. Sargent Jr.

[140] See, for example, CRS Report RL30914, *Federal Chief Information Officer (CIO): Opportunities and Challenges*, by Jeffrey W. Seifert.

[141] Prepared by Kristin M. Finklea, Coordinator, Analyst in Domestic Security (kfinklea@crs.loc.gov, 7-6259). See 18 U.S.C. §1001 nt. for classification details.

Major Relevant Provisions

- Made identity theft a federal crime.

- Provided penalties for individuals who either committed or attempted to commit identity theft.

- Provided for forfeiture of property used or intended to be used in the fraud.

- Directed the Federal Trade Commission (FTC) to record complaints of identity theft, provide victims with informational materials, and refer complaints to the appropriate consumer reporting and law enforcement agencies.[142]

Possible Updates

See "Identity Theft Penalty Enhancement Act" below.

Homeland Security Act of 2002 (HSA)

P.L. 107-296 (Titles II and III), 116 Stat. 2135.
6 U.S.C. §§121-195c, 441-444, and 481-486.[143]

Major Relevant Provisions

- Transferred some functions relating to the protection of information infrastructure from other agencies to the Department of Homeland Security (DHS).[144]

- Requires DHS to provide state and local governments and private entities with threat and vulnerability information, crisis-management support, and technical assistance relating to recovery plans for critical information systems.

- Permits the Secretary of Homeland Security to designate qualified technologies as subject to certain protections from liability in claims relating to their use in response to an act of terrorism.[145]

- Established mechanisms to facilitate information sharing among federal agencies and appropriate nonfederal government and critical-infrastructure personnel.[146]

---

[142] The FTC now records consumer complaint data and reports it in the Identity Theft Data Clearinghouse (Federal Trade Commission, "Reference Desk," *Fighting Back Against Identity Theft*, December 22, 2010, http://www.ftc.gov/bcp/edu/microsites/idtheft/reference-desk/index html); identity theft complaint data are available for 2000 and forward.

[143] For classification details, see 6 U.S.C. §101 nt.

[144] In particular, the act transferred to DHS the Federal Computer Incident Response Center, which had resided in the General Services Administration (GSA). In 2006, P.L. 109-295, The Department of Homeland Security Appropriations Act, 2007, established the position of Assistant Secretary for Cybersecurity and Communications (6 U.S.C. §321) within DHS but did not specify duties or responsibilities.

[145] This set of provisions (Subtitle G of Title VIII, 6 U.S.C. §441-444) is called the SAFETY Act.

[146] This set of provisions (Subtitle I of Title VIII, 6 U.S.C. §481-486) is called the Homeland Security Information Sharing Act. Sec. 486 was added by P.L. 109-90 and provides some liability protections relating to actions involving information sharing and analysis centers.

- Authorized DHS to establish a system of volunteer experts ("Net Guard") to assist local communities in responding to attacks on information and communications systems.

- Strengthened some criminal penalties relating to cybercrime.

- Created the Directorate of Science and Technology within DHS and assigned it broad R&D responsibilities, although responsibilities relating to cybersecurity R&D were not specifically described.

Possible Updates

Various concerns have been raised about the ways in which the act addressed cybersecurity, and a number of proposals have been made since its enactment to enhance the cybersecurity provisions. In the 111th Congress, the most comprehensive legislative proposal was in S. 3480, which was reported out of the Senate Committee on Homeland Security and Governmental Affairs in the 111th Congress, and reintroduced in the 112th Congress as S. 413 with minor modifications. It would add provisions on cybersecurity that would

- establish a center for cybersecurity and communications within DHS;

- require coordination with the DHS Office of Infrastructure Protection and sector-specific agencies;

- establish the United States Computer Emergency Readiness Team (US-CERT) within the center;

- stipulate information-sharing procedures for federal agencies and other entities;

- establish a program within the center to provide assistance to the private sector;

- require the center to identify cyber vulnerabilities to critical infrastructure and establish requirements to address them;

- establish procedures for response to imminent cyber threats to critical infrastructure,[147] enforcement of requirements, and protection of information; and

- require a risk-management strategy for security of the supply chain.

It would establish a cybersecurity R&D program in DHS and require coordination of those activities with other agencies and private entities. It would also establish a public/private-sector cybersecurity advisory council.

The *White House Proposal* would also substantially enhance DHS authority relating to cybersecurity. The proposal would differ in several ways from the approach taken by S. 413. Among other differences, it would provide enhanced authority to the DHS Secretary that S. 413 provides directly to a new center within the department. However, the *White House Proposal* would require the Secretary to establish a center with cybersecurity responsibilities for federal and critical infrastructure systems.[148] It also does not codify the establishment of US-CERT,

---

[147] See also "Communications Act of 1934" above.

[148] This center would presumably replace the federal incident center currently required under 44 U.S.C. 3546. The revision of the Federal Information Security Management Act of 2002 (FISMA) in the *White House Proposal* does not include the latter center.

---

unlike S. 413, and does not provide the President with the authority to implement emergency actions in response to an imminent risk to critical infrastructure. It does, however, provide the DHS Secretary with authority to direct responses of federal agencies to cybersecurity threats or incidents.

S. 2105 contains elements of both the *White House Proposal* and S. 413. It would establish a new center, with new authorities, but omits the provision in S. 413 establishing US-CERT by law, as well as the provision on presidential emergency powers. S. 2105 would require the Science and Technology Directorate of DHS to establish a cybersecurity R&D program. S. 1546 would also require departmental cybersecurity research.

H.R. 3674, as reported to the House, would provide additional responsibilities and authorities to DHS for the protection of federal information systems. It would provide for information sharing with federal and nonfederal entities, cybersecurity research and development (R&D), and recruitment and retention of cybersecurity personnel. To facilitate information sharing and technical assistance, it would create a center within DHS that would include a private-sector board of advisors. Unlike the bill as introduced, it does not include a nongovernmental clearinghouse for sharing cybersecurity information between the private sector and the federal government that was recommended by the *Task Force Report*. H.R. 3674 would also require DHS to perform cybersecurity R&D, to include testing, evaluation, and technology transfer.

Some other bills in the 111th Congress would also have revised the act. H.R. 6423, reintroduced as H.R. 174 in the 112th Congress, would establish a new office to develop, oversee, and enforce cybersecurity compliance for critical infrastructure sectors. H.R. 266, reintroduced as H.R. 76, would add a cybersecurity fellowship program for nonfederal officials to familiarize them with DHS cybersecurity activities. H.R. 4507 and H.R. 4842 would have added a cybersecurity training initiative for first responders and others. H.R. 2868 and S. 3599 would have added chemical-facility security measures, including cybersecurity, to the act.

See also "DHS Authorities for Protection of Federal Systems," "Cybersecurity Workforce," "Research and Development," "Protection of Privately Held Critical Infrastructure (CI)," and "Information Sharing."

Federal Information Security Management Act of 2002 (FISMA)

P.L. 107-296 (Title X), 116 Stat. 2259.
P.L. 107-347 (Title III), 116 Stat. 2946.
44 U.S.C. Chapter 35, Subchapters II and III, [40 U.S.C. 11331, 15 U.S.C. 278g-3 & 4].[149]

Major Relevant Provisions

FISMA created a security framework for federal information systems, with an emphasis on risk management, and gave specific responsibilities to the Office of Management and Budget (OMB),

---

[149] FISMA was originally enacted as part of the Homeland Security Act of 2002, replacing provisions enacted by the Floyd D. Spence National Defense Authorization Act for Fiscal Year 2001 (P.L. 106-398, Title X, Subtitle G), enacted in 2000 but with a 2002 sunset. FISMA was reenacted in the same Congress by the E-government Act. Subchapter II is not in effect. The title 40 provision was originally enacted as part of the Clinger-Cohen Act (see p. 38), and the title 15 provisions are part of the NIST Act (see p. 23). See footnote 151 for more detail.

the National Institute of Standards and Technology (NIST), and the heads, chief information officers (CIOs), chief information security officers (CISOs), and inspector generals (IGs) of federal agencies.[150]

- Required executive agencies to inventory major computer systems, identify and provide appropriate security protections, and develop, document, and implement agency-wide information security programs.

- Gave OMB responsibility for overseeing federal information-security policy and evaluating agency information-security programs, but exempted national security systems, except with respect to enforcement of accountability for meeting requirements and reporting to Congress.

- Revised the responsibilities of the Secretary of Commerce and NIST for information-system standards and transferred responsibility for promulgation of those standards from the Secretary of Commerce to OMB.[151]

- Required that NIST cybersecurity standards be complementary with those developed for national security systems, to the extent feasible.

- Required heads of federal agencies to provide security protections commensurate with risk and to comply with applicable security standards. Specifically required agencies using national security systems to provide security protections commensurate with risk and in compliance with standards for such systems.

- Required senior agency officials to perform risk assessments, to determine and implement necessary security controls in a cost-effective manner, and to evaluate those controls periodically.

- Designated specific information-security responsibilities for agencies' chief information security officers, including agency-wide information-security programs, policies, and procedures, and training of security and other personnel.

- Required designation of an information-security officer in each agency, security awareness training, processes for remedial action to address deficiencies, and procedures for handling security incidents and ensuring continuity of operations.

---

[150] For a more detailed description, see, for example, Government Accountability Office, *Information Security: Weaknesses Continue Amid New Federal Efforts to Implement Requirements*, GAO-12-137, October 2011, http://www.gao.gov/new.items/d12137.pdf.

[151] The standards-promulgation authority had been granted to the Secretary of Commerce under the Clinger-Cohen Act of 1996 (P.L. 104-106) but was transferred to the Director of OMB by the FISMA title in the HSA in 2002 (P.L. 107-296, Sec. 1002, 40 U.S.C. 11331). The version of the main Chapter 35 currently in effect (Subchapter III) was enacted by the FISMA title in the E-Government Act of 2002 (P.L. 107-347, Title III), which suspended Subchapter II, which had been revised by the HSA. That is not the case for 40 U.S.C. 11331, for which the P.L. 107-347 version would have retained the authority of the Secretary of Commerce to promulgate those standards as established in the Clinger-Cohen Act of 1996 (see p. 38), even though the E-Government Act was enacted after the HSA. Similarly, the revision to the NIST Act at 15 U.S.C. 278g-3 & 4 is that made by the HSA. The reason for this potentially confusing difference appears to be that (1) the effective date of HSA was later than that of the E-Government Act, and (2) HSA amended the existing subchapter II of 44 U.S.C. Chapter 35; the E-Government Act explicitly suspended that subchapter. In contrast, the revisions both laws made to the Paperwork Reduction Act, adding a subsection (c) to 44 U.S.C. §3505 (requiring inventories of federal information systems) were codified. However, there appear to remain some ambiguities in interpretation of the applicability of the two acts, which would presumably be resolved if FISMA is revised.

- Required annual agency reports to Congress, performance plans, and independent evaluations of information security.

- Established a central federal incident center, overseen by OMB, to analyze incidents and provide technical assistance relating to them, to inform agency operators about current and potential threats and vulnerabilities, and to consult with NIST, NSA, and other appropriate agencies about incidents.

- Gave responsibility for protection of mission-crucial systems in DOD and the CIA to the Secretary of Defense and the DCI, respectively, and required the Secretary of Defense to include compliance with the provisions above in developing program strategies for the Defense Information Assurance Program (10 U.S.C. §2224).

Possible Updates

A commonly expressed concern about FISMA is that it is awkward and inefficient in providing adequate cybersecurity to government IT systems. The causes cited have varied but common themes have included inadequate resources, a focus on procedure and reporting rather than operational security, lack of widely accepted cybersecurity metrics, variations in agency interpretation of the mandates in the act, excessive focus on individual information systems as opposed to the agency's overall information architecture, and insufficient means to enforce compliance both within and across agencies.[152] Several legislative proposals in the 111th and 112th Congresses have included major revisions to the act. The proposals varied in detail, with several notable provisions in some:

- Creation of a White House office with responsibility for cybersecurity;

- Transfer of responsibilities from OMB to the Secretary of Homeland Security or the Secretary of Commerce;

- Revisions to agency responsibilities under the act, including continuous monitoring, use of metrics, and emphasis on risk-based rather than minimum security measures;

- Changes in reporting requirements;

- Specification of cybersecurity requirements for acquisitions and the IT supply chain; and

- Establishment of mechanisms for interagency collaboration on cybersecurity.

---

[152] See, for example, S.Rept. 111-368, and House Subcommittee on Government Management, Organization, and Procurement, *The State of Federal Information Security, Committee on Oversight and Government Reform* (Washington, DC: U.S. Government Printing Office, 2009), http://www.gpo.gov/fdsys/pkg/CHRG-111hhrg57125/pdf/ CHRG-111hhrg57125.pdf. OMB has recently attempted to address some of the operational issues administratively by delegating some responsibilities to DHS (Orszag and Schmidt, "Clarifying Cybersecurity Responsibilities and Activities of the Executive Office of the President and the Department of Homeland Security (DHS)"). Weaknesses in FISMA implementation have been cited repeatedly by GAO in reports required by the act (see, for example, Government Accountability Office, *Information Security: Weaknesses Continue Amid New Federal Efforts to Implement Requirements*).

In the 111th Congress, H.R. 5136 passed in the House,[153] and S. 3480 was reported out of the Senate Homeland Security and Governmental Affairs Committee.

In the 112th Congress, the *Task Force Report* recommends an increased focus on monitoring, support for DHS authority, and taking new and emerging technologies, such as cloud computing, into account.[154] H.R. 1136 would make many changes similar to those in H.R. 5136 in the 111th Congress, transferring responsibility to a new White House Office for Cyberspace created by the bill. H.R. 4257, in contrast, retains the current role of the OMB Director. H.R. 4257 passed the House under suspension of the rules in April 2012.

S. 413 would make changes similar to those in S. 3480 in the previous Congress, transferring responsibility for federal information security policy from the Director of OMB to the Director of a new DHS center that the bill would establish. The *White House Proposal* is broadly similar to congressional proposals in many details. However, it would not create a White House cybersecurity office and would transfer responsibilities to the DHS Secretary rather than to a new cybersecurity center within DHS. S. 2105 includes a similar approach. S. 2151 and S. 3342, in contrast, would transfer responsibilities from OMB to the Secretary of Commerce.

S. 1535 would require that agency information security programs assess the practices of contractors and third parties with respect to sensitive personally identifiable information as defined in the bill and ensure that any deficiencies are remediated.

See also "FISMA Reform."

Terrorism Risk Insurance Act of 2002

P.L. 107-297, 116 Stat. 2322.
15 U.S.C. §6701 nt.[155]

Major Relevant Provisions

- Provides federal cost-sharing subsidies for insured losses resulting from acts of terrorism.

Possible Updates

The act is intended to provide incentives for the development of insurance coverage for losses from acts of terrorism. Losses from cyber attacks are not specifically included, and some observers have raised concerns about whether some modification of the act would be appropriate.[156]

---

[153] The bill included provisions from H.R. 4900, which was ordered reported by the House Oversight and Government Reform Committee.

[154] House Republican Cybersecurity Task Force, *Recommendations*, p. 13.

[155] The original act was amended by P.L. 109-144, the Terrorism Risk Extension Act of 1995, and P.L. 110-160, the Terrorism Risk Insurance Program Reauthorization Act of 2007. For classification details, see 15 U.S.C. 6701 nt.

[156] See, for example, Karen C. Yotis, "TRIA and the Perils of Terrorism Insurance," *Viewpoint*, Summer 2007, http://www.aaisonline.com/viewpoint/07sum6 html.

Cyber Security Research and Development Act, 2002

P.L. 107-305, 116 Stat. 2367,
15 U.S.C. [§§278g,h], §7401 et seq.[157]

Major Relevant Provisions

- Requires the National Science Foundation (NSF) to award grants for basic research to enhance computer security and for improving undergraduate and master's degree programs, doctoral research, and faculty development programs in computer and network security; and to establish multidisciplinary centers for research on computer and network security.

- Requires NIST to establish programs to award postdoctoral and senior research fellowships in cybersecurity and to assist institutions of higher learning that partner with for-profit entities to perform cybersecurity research; to perform intramural specified cybersecurity research; and to develop a checklist of security settings for federal computer hardware and software for voluntary use by federal agencies.

Possible Updates

A commonly expressed concern about federal research and development (R&D) relating to cybersecurity has been that it is insufficiently coordinated and prioritized, and focuses too little on understanding of fundamental principles and using them to develop transformational technologies. The George W. Bush Administration attempted to address the latter gap through the "leap-ahead" technology component of the Comprehensive Cybersecurity Initiative.[158] The Obama Administration's policy review[159] also called for expanded, transformational research.

Concerns have also been raised about the need to improve the process by which NIST creates checklists and other guidance and technical standards for federal IT systems.[160]

H.R. 4061 in the 111th Congress would have addressed those concerns by revising the act. A similar bill in the 112th Congress, H.R. 2096, would, as amended, expand NSF R&D programs in cybersecurity, and require NIST to develop automated security specifications for its cybersecurity standards, checklists, and associated data. S. 2105, S. 2151, and S. 3342 would also expand cybersecurity topics addressed by NSF.

---

[157] 15 U.S.C. §§278g,h are part of the NIST Act (see p. 23).

[158] See, for example, NITRD, "About the NITRD Program: National Cyber Leap Year", July 22, 2009, http://www.nitrd.gov/leapyear/index.aspx.

[159] The White House, *Cyberspace Policy Review*.

[160] See, for example, H.Rept. 111-405, CSIS Commission on Cybersecurity for the 44th Presidency, *A Human Capital Crisis in Cybersecurity*, July 2010, http://csis.org/files/publication/100720_Lewis_HumanCapital_WEB_BlkWhteVersion.pdf.

E-Government Act of 2002

P.L. 107-347, 116 Stat. 2899.
5 U.S.C. Chapter 37, 44 U.S.C. 3501 nt., 44 U.S.C. Chapter 35, Subchapter 2, and Chapter 36.

Major Relevant Provisions

Serves as the primary legislative vehicle to guide federal IT management and initiatives to make information and services available online. Significant provisions include the following:

- Established the Office of Electronic Government within OMB, to be headed by an administrator with a range of IT management responsibilities, including cybersecurity.

- Established the interagency CIO (Chief Information Officer) Council and specified working with the National Institute of Standards and Technology (NIST) on security standards as one of its functions.

- Assigned agency CIOs responsibility for monitoring implementation of federal cybersecurity standards in their agencies.

- Contains various other requirements for security and protection of confidential information, including electronic authentication and privacy guidelines.

- Established a five-year personnel exchange program between federal agencies and private sector organizations to help agencies fill IT management training needs.

- Also included the "Federal Information Security Management Act of 2002 (FISMA)."

Possible Update

The *White House Proposal* would renew the personnel exchange program, which terminated at the end of 2007, and remove the current restriction in eligibility to management personnel. While this program would be applicable to any subdiscipline of IT, a widely held belief at present is that gaps in cybersecurity expertise are of particular concern. S. 1732 would revise the privacy provisions to account for the increased commercial availability of personally identifiable information, which the bill defines broadly.[161] It would also require agencies to designate chief privacy officers and create a council of them, and broaden OMB's privacy responsibilities.

---

[161] It would include "any information about an individual maintained by an agency."

Identity Theft Penalty Enhancement Act

P.L. 108-275, 118 Stat. 831.
18 U.S.C. §§1028, 1028A.[162]

Major Relevant Provisions

- Established penalties for *aggravated* identity theft, in which a convicted perpetrator could receive additional penalties (two to five years' imprisonment) for identity theft committed in relation to other federal crimes.[163]

Possible Updates

While the number of reported incidents of identity theft fell in 2010, identity theft has generally been the fastest growing type of fraud in the United States over the past decade.[164] FTC complaint data indicate that the most common fraud complaint received (19% of all consumer fraud complaints in 2010) has remained that of identity theft.[165] In 2010, for instance, about 8.1 million Americans were reportedly victims of identity theft. This is a decrease of about 28% from the approximately 11.1 million who were victimized in 2009.[166] Javelin Strategy and Research estimates that identity theft cost consumers about $37 billion in 2010.

The most recent congressional action taken to enhance the identity theft laws was through the Identity Theft Enforcement and Restitution Act of 2008 (Title II of P.L. 110-326). Among other elements, several of which were recommended by a presidential task force in 2007,[167] the act authorized restitution to identity theft victims for their time spent recovering from the harm caused by the actual or intended identity theft. Legislation has not yet, however, adopted recommendations of the task force to

- amend the identity theft and aggravated identity theft statutes so that thieves who misappropriate the identities of corporations and organizations—and not just the identities of individuals—can be prosecuted,[168] and

- amend the aggravated identity theft statute by adding new crimes as predicate offenses[169] for aggravated identity theft violations.[170]

---

[162] Prepared by Kristin M. Finklea, Analyst in Domestic Security (kfinklea@crs.loc.gov, 7-6259). For classification details, see 18 U.S.C. §1028 nt.

[163] Examples of such federal crimes include theft of public property, theft by a bank officer or employee, theft from employee benefit plans, false statements regarding Social Security and Medicare benefits, several fraud and immigration offenses, and specified felony violations pertaining to terrorist acts.

[164] For more information on identity theft, see CRS Report R40599, *Identity Theft: Trends and Issues*, by Kristin M. Finklea.

[165] Federal Trade Commission, *Consumer Sentinel Network Data Book for January–December, 2010*, March 2010, http://www.ftc.gov/sentinel/reports/sentinel-annual-reports/sentinel-cy2010.pdf.

[166] Javelin Strategy & Research, *2011 Identity Fraud Survey Report: Consumer Version*, February 2011, p. 5 (available at https://www.javelinstrategy.com/brochure/207).

[167] The President's Identity Theft Task Force, *Combating Identity Theft: A Strategic Plan*, April 2007, http://www.identitytheft.gov/reports/StrategicPlan.pdf.

[168] This would involve revision of 18 U.S.C. §§1028 and 1028A.

[169] A predicate offense can be described as a crime that is a component of a more serious offense. For example, in the (continued...)

The task force recommended that Congress clarify the identity theft and aggravated identity theft statutes to cover both individuals and organizations targeted by identity thieves because the range of potential victims includes not only individuals but organizations as well. The task force cites "phishing" as a means by which identity thieves assume the identity of a corporation or organization in order to solicit personally identifiable information from individuals.[171]

In part because identity theft is a facilitating crime, and the criminal act of stealing someone's identity often does not end there, investigating and prosecuting identity theft often involves investigating and prosecuting a number of related crimes. In light of this interconnectivity, the task force recommended expanding the list of predicate offenses for aggravated identity theft. The task force specifically suggested adding identity theft-related crimes such as mail theft,[172] counterfeit securities,[173] and tax fraud.[174]

The *Task Force Report* also recommends requiring restitution for victims of identity theft and computer fraud.[175] At present, the statute authorizes restitution but does not require it.

Intelligence Reform and Terrorism Prevention Act of 2004 (IRTPA)

P.L. 108-458, 118 Stat. 3638.
42 U.S.C. §2000ee, 50 U.S.C. §403-1 et seq., §403-3 et seq., §404o et. seq.[176]

Major Relevant Provisions

- Established the position of the Director of National Intelligence.

- Establishes mission responsibilities for some entities in the intelligence, homeland security, and national security communities.

- Discusses issues related to the collection, analysis, and sharing of security-related information.

- Establishes a Privacy and Civil Liberties Board within the Executive Office of the President.

Possible Updates

The act does not contain a single reference to cyber, cybersecurity, or related activities. Its stated purpose is to "reform the intelligence community and the intelligence and intelligence-related

---

(...continued)

case of money laundering, the crime that produces the funds that are to be laundered is the predicate offense.

[170] This would involve revision of 18 U.S.C. §1028A.

[171] The President's Identity Theft Task Force, *Combating Identity Theft: A Strategic Plan*, pp. 91 – 92.

[172] 18 U.S.C. §1708.

[173] 18 U.S.C. §513.

[174] 26 U.S.C. §7201, 7206-7207.

[175] House Republican Cybersecurity Task Force, *Recommendations*, p. 14.

[176] Prepared by John Rollins, Specialist in Terrorism and National Security (jrollins@crs.loc.gov, 7-5529). Classification of this act is complex. For details, see 50 U.S.C. §401 nt.

activities of the United States Government, and for other purposes." The act contains findings and recommendations offered in the 9/11 Commission Report[177] and other assessments that address national and homeland security shortcomings associated with the terrorist attacks of September 11, 2001.

Numerous organizations, programs, and activities in the act currently address cybersecurity-related issues. IRPTA addresses many types of risks to the nation and threats emanating from man-made and naturally occurring events. The broad themes of the act could be categorized as how the federal government identifies, assesses, defeats, responds to, and recovers from current and emerging threats. The act might be updated to incorporate cybersecurity-related issues. However, any such update could affect numerous organizations and activities. [178]

---

[177] National Commission on Terrorist Attacks Upon the United States , *The 9/11 Commission Report*, July 22, 2004, http://www.9-11commission.gov/report/911Report.pdf.

[178] For more information on threats, responses, and issues associated with cyberterrorism, see CRS Report R41674, *Terrorist Use of the Internet: Information Operations in Cyberspace*, by Catherine A. Theohary and John Rollins.

Table 2. Laws Identified as Having Relevant Cybersecurity Provisions

Year	Popular Name	Law	Stat.	U.S.C.	Applicability and Notes	CRS Reports
6/18/1878	*Posse Comitatus Act (p. 20)*	Ch. 263	20 Stat. 152	18 U.S.C. §1385	Restricts the use of military forces in civilian law enforcement within the United States. May prevent assistance to civil agencies that lack DOD expertise and capabilities.	RS20590
7/2/1890 and later	*Antitrust Laws: (p. 21)*					
	Sherman Antitrust Act, *Wilson Tariff Act* *Clayton Act* Sec. 5 of the Federal Trade Commission (FTC) Act	Ch. 647 Ch. 349, §73 P.L. 63-212 Ch, 311, §5	26 Stat. 209 28 Stat. 570 38 Stat. 730 38 Stat. 719	15 U.S.C. §§1-7 15 U.S.C. §§8-11 15 U.S.C. §§12-27 15 U.S.C. §45(a)	"Antitrust laws" generally means the three laws listed in 15 U.S.C. §12(a) and Sec. 5 of the FTC Act, which forbid combinations or agreements that unreasonably restrain trade. May create barriers to sharing of information or collaboration to enhance cybersecurity among private sector entities.	
3/3/1901	*National Institute of Standards and Technology (NIST) Act (p. 23)*	Ch. 872	31 Stat. 1449	15 U.S.C. §271 et seq.	The original act gave the agency responsibilities relating to technical standards. Later amendments established a computer standards program and specified research topics, among them computer and telecommunication systems, including information security and control systems.	
8/13/1912	Radio Act of 1912	Ch. 287	37 Stat. 302		Established a radio licensing regime and regulated private radio communications, creating a precedent for wireless regulation. Repealed by the Radio Act of 1927.	
6/10/1920	*Federal Power Act (p. 23)*	Ch. 285	41 Stat. 1063	16 U.S.C. §791a et seq., §824 et seq.	Established the Federal Energy Regulatory Commission (FERC) and gave it regulatory authority over interstate sale and transmission of electric power. The move toward a national smart grid is raising concerns about vulnerability to cyber attack.	R41886

Year	Popular Name	Law	Stat.	U.S.C.	Applicability and Notes	CRS Reports
2/23/1927	Radio Act of 1927	Ch. 169	44 Stat. 1162		Created the Federal Radio Commission as an independent agency (predecessor of the FCC) and outlawed interception and divulging private radio messages. Repealed by the Communications Act of 1934 (see p. 24).	
6/19/1934	*Communications Act of 1934 (p.24)*	Ch. 652	48 Stat. 1064	47 U.S.C. §151 et seq.	Established the Federal Communications Commission (FCC) and gave it regulatory authority over both domestic and international commercial wired and wireless communications. Provides the President with emergency powers over communications stations and devices. Governs protection by cable operators of information about subscribers.	RL32589 RL34693
7/26/1947	*National Security Act of 1947 (p. 25)*	Ch. 343	61 Stat. 495	50 U.S.C. §401 et seq.	Provided the basis for the modern organization of U.S. defense and national security by reorganizing military and intelligence functions in the federal government. Created the National Security Council, the Central Intelligence Agency, and the position of Secretary of Defense. Established procedures for access to classified information.	
1/27/1948	*US Information and Educational Exchange Act of 1948 (Smith-Mundt Act) (p. 25)*	Ch. 36	62 Stat. 6	22 U.S.C. §1431 et seq.	Restricts the State Department from disseminating public diplomacy information domestically and limits its authority to communicate with the American public in general. Has been interpreted by some to prohibit the military from conducting cyberspace information operations, some of which could be considered propaganda that could reach U.S. citizens, since the government does not restrict Internet access according to territorial boundaries.	R41674

Year	Popular Name	Law	Stat.	U.S.C.	Applicability and Notes	CRS Reports
9/8/1950	Defense Production Act of 1950	Ch. 932	64 Stat. 798	50 U.S.C. App. §2061 et seq.	Codifies a robust legal authority given the President to force industry to give priority to national security production and ensure the survival of security-critical domestic production capacities. It is also the statutory underpinning of governmental review of foreign investment in U.S. companies.	RS20587 RL31133
8/1/1956	*State Department Basic Authorities Act of 1956 (p. 27)*	P.L. 84-885	70 Stat. 890	22 U.S.C. §2651a	Specifies the organization of the Department of State, including the positions of coordinator for counterterrorism. As the Internet becomes increasingly international, concerns have been raised about the development and coordination of international efforts in cybersecurity by the United States.	R40989
10/30/1965	Brooks Automatic Data Processing Act	P.L. 89-306	79 Stat. 1127		Gave GSA authority over acquisition of automatic data processing equipment by federal agencies, and gave NIST responsibilities for developing standards and guidelines relating to automatic data processing and federal computer systems. Repealed by the Clinger-Cohen Act of 1996 (see p. 38).	
7/4/1966	*Freedom of Information Act (FOIA) (p. 27)*	P.L. 89-487	80 Stat. 250	5 U.S.C. §552	Enables anyone to access agency records except those falling into nine categories of exemption, among them classified documents, those exempted by specific statutes, and trade secrets or other confidential commercial or financial information.	R41406 R41933
6/19/1968	*Omnibus Crime Control and Safe Streets Act of 1968 (p. 29)*	P.L. 90-351	82 Stat. 197	42 U.S.C. Chapter 46, §§3701 to 3797ee-1	Title I established federal grant programs and other forms of assistance to state and local law enforcement. Title III is a comprehensive wiretapping and electronic eavesdropping statute that not only outlawed both activities in general terms but that also permitted federal and state law enforcement officers to use them under strict limitations.	

Year	Popular Name	Law	Stat.	U.S.C.	Applicability and Notes	CRS Reports
10/15/1970	*Racketeer Influenced and Corrupt Organizations Act (RICO) (p. 29)*	P.L. 91-452	84 Stat. 941	18 U.S.C. Chapter 96, §§1961-1968	Enlarges the civil and criminal consequences of a list of state and federal crimes when committed in a way characteristic of the conduct of organized crime (racketeering).	96-950
10/6/1972	*Federal Advisory Committee Act (p. 30)*	P.L. 92-463	86 Stat. 770	5 U.S.C. App., §§1-16	Specifies conditions for establishing a federal advisory committee and its responsibilities and limitations. Requires open, public meetings and that records be available for public inspection. Has been criticized as potentially impeding the development of public/private partnerships in cybersecurity, particularly private-sector communications and input on policy.	R40520
11/7/1973	War Powers Resolution	P.L. 93-148	87 Stat. 555	50 U.S.C. Chapter 33, §§1541-1548.	Establishes procedures to circumscribe presidential authority to use armed forces in potential or actual hostilities without congressional authorization.	R41199 R41989
12/31/1974	*Privacy Act of 1974 (p. 30)*	P.L. 93-579	88 Stat. 1896	5 U.S.C. §552a	Limits the disclosure of personally identifiable information (PII) held by federal agencies. Established a code of fair information practices for collection, management, and dissemination of records by agencies, including requirements for security and confidentiality of records.	
10/25/1978	Foreign Intelligence Surveillance Act of 1978 (FISA)	P.L. 95-511	92 Stat. 1783	18 U.S.C. §§2511, 2518-9, 50 U.S.C. Chapter 36, §§1801-1885c	In foreign intelligence investigations, provides a statutory framework for federal agencies to obtain authorization to conduct electronic surveillance, utilize pen registers and trap and trace devices, or access specified records.	98-326 R40138
10/13/1980	Privacy Protection Act of 1980	P.L. 96-440	94 Stat. 1879	42 U.S.C. Chapter 21A, §§2000aa-5 to 2000aa-12	Protects journalists from being required to turn over to law enforcement any work product and documentary materials, including sources, before dissemination to the public.	

Year	Popular Name	Law	Stat.	U.S.C.	Applicability and Notes	CRS Reports
10/12/1984	*Counterfeit Access Device and Computer Fraud and Abuse Act of 1984 (p. 31)*	P.L. 98-473	98 Stat. 2190	18 U.S.C. §1030	Provided criminal penalties for unauthorized access and use of computers and networks. Part of the Comprehensive Crime Control Act of 1984.	97-1025
10/16/1986	Computer Fraud and Abuse Act of 1986	P.L. 99-474	100 Stat. 1213	18 U.S.C. §1030	Expanded the scope of the Counterfeit Access Device and Computer Fraud and Abuse Act of 1984. For government computers, criminalized electronic trespassing, exceeding authorized access, and destroying information; also criminalized trafficking in stolen computer passwords. Created a statutory exemption for intelligence and law enforcement activities.	
10/21/1986	*Electronic Communications Privacy Act of 1986 (ECPA) (p. 32)*	P.L. 99-508	100 Stat. 1848	18 U.S.C. §§2510-2522, 2701-2712, 3121-3126	Attempts to strike a balance between privacy rights and the needs of law enforcement with respect to data shared or stored by electronic and telecommunications services. Unless otherwise provided, prohibits the interception of or access to stored oral or electronic communications, use or disclosure of information so obtained, or possession of electronic eavesdropping equipment.	R41733 R41756 RL34693
10/30/1986	*Department of Defense Appropriations Act, 1987 (p. 34)*	P.L. 99-591	100 Stat. 3341-82, 3341-122	10 U.S.C. §167	Established unified combatant command for special operations forces, including the U.S. Strategic Command, under which the U.S. Cyber Command was organized.	
1/8/1988	Computer Security Act of 1987	P.L. 100-235	101 Stat. 1724	15 U.S.C. §§272, 278g-3, 278g-4, 278h	Required NIST to develop and the Secretary of Commerce to promulgate security standards and guidelines for federal computer systems except national security systems. Also required agency planning and training in computer security (this provision was superseded by FISMA—see p. 42).	
10/18/1988	Computer Matching and Privacy Protection Act of 1988	P.L. 100-503	102 Stat. 2507	5 U.S.C. §552a	Amended the Privacy Act (see p. 30), establishing procedural safeguards for use of computer matching on records covered by the act.	

Year	Popular Name	Law	Stat.	U.S.C.	Applicability and Notes	CRS Reports
12/9/1991	*High Performance Computing Act of 1991 (p. 34)*	P.L. 102-194	105 Stat. 1594	15 U.S.C. Chapter 81	Established a federal high-performance computing program and requires that it address security needs and provide for interagency coordination.	RL33586
10/25/1994	*Communications Assistance for Law Enforcement Act (CALEA) of 1994 (p. 36)*	P.L. 103-414	108 Stat. 4279	47 U.S.C. §1001 et seq.	Requires telecommunications carriers to assist law enforcement in performing electronic surveillance and directs the telecommunications industry to design, develop, and deploy solutions that meet requirements for carriers to support authorized electronic surveillance.	RL30677
5/25/1995	Paperwork Reduction Act of 1995	P.L. 104-13	109 Stat. 163	44 U.S.C. Chapter 35, §§3501-3549	Gave the Office of Management and Budget (OMB) authority to develop information-resource management polices and standards, required consultation with NIST and GSA on information technology (IT), and required agencies to implement processes relating to information security and privacy.	
2/8/1996	Telecommunications Act of 1996	P.L. 104-104	110 Stat. 56	See 47 U.S.C. §609 nt. for affected provisions.	Overhauled telecommunications law, including significant deregulation of U.S. telecommunications markets, eliminating regulatory barriers to competition.	
2/8/1996	*Communications Decency Act of 1996 (p. 37)*	P.L. 104-104 (Title V)	110 Stat. 133	See 47 U.S.C. §§223, 230	Intended to regulate indecency and obscenity on telecommunications systems, including the Internet. Has been interpreted to absolve Internet service providers and certain web-based services of responsibility for third-party content residing on those networks or websites.	R41499

Year	Popular Name	Law	Stat.	U.S.C.	Applicability and Notes	CRS Reports
2/10/1996	*Clinger-Cohen Act (Information Technology Management Reform Act) of 1996) (p. 38)*	P.L. 104-106, (Div. D and E)	110 Stat. 642	40 U.S.C. §11001 et seq.	Required agencies to ensure adequacy of information-security policies, OMB to oversee major IT acquisitions, and the Secretary of Commerce to promulgate compulsory federal computer standards based on those developed by NIST. Exempted national security systems from most provisions.	
8/21/1996	Health Insurance Portability and Accountability Act of 1996 (HIPAA)	P.L. 104-191	110 Stat. 1936	42 U.S.C. §1320d et seq.	Required the Secretary of Health and Human Services to establish security standards and regulations for protecting the privacy of individually identifiable health information, and required covered health-care entities to protect the security of such information.	RL34120
10/11/1996	Economic Espionage Act of 1996	P.L. 104-294	110 Stat. 3488	18 U.S.C. §1030, Chapter 90, §§1831-1839	Outlaws theft of trade secret information, including electronically stored information, if "reasonable measures" have been taken to keep it secret. Also contains the National Information Infrastructure Protection Act of 1996, amending 18 U.S.C. §1030 (see the Counterfeit Access Device and Computer Fraud and Abuse Act of 1984, p. 31), broadening prohibited activities relating to unauthorized access to computers.	
10/30/1998	*Identity Theft and Assumption Deterrence Act of 1998 (p. 39)*	P.L. 105-318	112 Stat. 3007	18 U.S.C. §1028	Made identity theft a federal crime, provides penalties, and directed the FTC to record and refer complaints.	R40599
10/5/1999	National Defense Authorization Act for Fiscal Year 2000	P.L. 106-65	113 Stat. 512	10 U.S.C. §2224	Established the Defense Information Assurance Program and required development of a testbed and coordination with other federal agencies.	
11/12/1999	Gramm-Leach-Bliley Act of 1999	P.L. 106-102 (Title V)	113 Stat. 1338	15 U.S.C. Chapter 94, §§6801-6827	Requires financial institutions to protect the security and confidentiality of customers' personal information; authorized regulations for that purpose.	RL34120 RS20185

Year	Popular Name	Law	Stat.	U.S.C.	Applicability and Notes	CRS Reports
10/30/2000	Floyd D. Spence National Defense Authorization Act for Fiscal Year 2001	P.L. 106-398 (Titles IX & X)	114 STAT. 1654A–233; 1654A–266	10 U.S.C. Chapter 112, §§2200-2200f	Established the DOD information assurance scholarship program; set cybersecurity requirements for federal systems superseded by FISMA in 2002	
10/26/2001	USA PATRIOT Act of 2001	P.L. 107-56	115 Stat. 272	see 18 U.S.C. §1 nt. and classification tables.[a]	Authorized various law-enforcement activities relating to computer fraud and abuse.	R40980
7/30/2002	Sarbanes-Oxley Act of 2002	P.L. 107-204	116 Stat. 745	15 U.S.C. §7262	Requires annual reporting on internal financial controls of covered firms to the Securities and Exchange Commission (SEC). Such controls typically include information security.	
11/25/2002	*Homeland Security Act of 2002 (HSA) (p. 40)*	P.L. 107-296 (Titles II and III)	116 Stat. 2135	6 U.S.C. §§121-195c, 441-444, and 481-486	Created the Department of Homeland Security (DHS) and gave it functions relating to the protection of information infrastructure, including providing state and local governments and private entities with threat and vulnerability information, crisis-management support, and technical assistance. Strengthened some criminal penalties relating to cybercrime.	
11/25/2002	*Federal Information Security Management Act of 2002 (FISMA) (p. 42)*	P.L. 107-296 (Title X) P.L. 107-347 (Title III)	116 Stat. 2259 116 Stat. 2946	44 U.S.C. Chapter 35, Subchapters II and III, 40 U.S.C. 11331, 15 U.S.C. 278g-3 & 4	Created a cybersecurity framework for federal information systems, with an emphasis on risk management, and required implementation of agency-wide information security programs. Gave oversight responsibility to OMB, revised the responsibilities of the Secretary of Commerce and NIST for information-system standards, and transferred responsibility for promulgation of those standards from the Secretary of Commerce to OMB.	
11/26/2002	*Terrorism Risk Insurance Act of 2002 (p. 45)*	P.L. 107-297	116 Stat. 2322	15 U.S.C. §6701 nt.	Provides federal cost-sharing subsidies for insured losses resulting from acts of terrorism.	

Year	Popular Name	Law	Stat.	U.S.C.	Applicability and Notes	CRS Reports
11/27/2002	*Cyber Security Research and Development Act, 2002 (p. 45)*	P.L. 107-305	116 Stat. 2367	15 U.S.C. §§278g, h, 7401 et seq.	Requires the National Science Foundation (NSF) to award grants for basic research and education to enhance computer security. Required NIST to establish cybersecurity research programs.	
12/17/2002	*E-Government Act of 2002 (p. 47)*	P.L. 107-347	116 Stat. 2899	5 U.S.C. Chapter 37, 44 U.S.C. §3501 nt., Chapter 35, Subchapter 2, and Chapter 36	Serves as the primary legislative vehicle to guide federal IT management and initiatives to make information and services available online. Established the Office of Electronic Government within OMB, the Chief Information Officers (CIO) Council, and a government/private-sector personnel exchange program; includes FISMA; established and contains various other requirements for security and protection of confidential information.	
12/4/2003	Fair and Accurate Credit Transactions Act of 2003	P.L. 108-159	117 Stat. 1952	See 15 U.S.C. §1601 nt. for affected provisions.	Required the FTC and other agencies to develop guidelines for identity theft prevention programs in financial institutions, including "red flags" indicating possible identity theft.	RS20185
12/16/2003	Controlling the Assault of Non-Solicited Pornography and Marketing (CAN-SPAM) Act of 2003	P.L. 108-187	117 Stat. 2699	15 U.S.C. Chapter 103, §§7701-7713, 18 U.S.C. 1037	Imposed regulations on the transmission of unsolicited commercial email, including prohibitions against predatory and abusive email, and false or misleading transmission of information.	
7/15/2004	*Identity Theft Penalty Enhancement Act 2004 (p. 48)*	P.L. 108-275	118 Stat. 831	18 U.S.C. §§1028, 1028A	Established penalties for aggravated identity theft.	R40599
12/17/2004	*Intelligence Reform and Terrorism Prevention Act of 2004 (IRPTA) (p. 49)*	P.L. 108-458	118 Stat. 3638	42 U.S. C. §2000ee, 50 U.S.C. §403-1 et seq., §403-3 et seq., §404o et. seq.	Created the position of Director of National Intelligence (DNI). Established mission responsibilities for some entities in the intelligence, homeland security, and national security communities, and established a Privacy and Civil Liberties Board within the Executive Office of the President.	

Year	Popular Name	Law	Stat.	U.S.C.	Applicability and Notes	CRS Reports
8/8/2005	Energy Policy Act of 2005 (EPACT)	P.L. 109-58	119 Stat. 594	16 U.S.C. 824o	Requires FERC to certify an Electric Reliability Organization (ERO) to establish and enforce reliability standards for bulk electric-power system facilities.	R41886
10/4/2006	Department of Homeland Security Appropriations Act, 2007	P.L. 109-295	120 Stat. 1355	6 U.S.C. §121 nt.	Sec. 550 required the Secretary of Homeland Security to issue regulations (6 C.F.R. Part 27) establishing risk-based performance standards for security of chemical facilities; regulations include cybersecurity standards requirement (6 C.F.R. §27.230(a)(8)).	
8/5/2007	Protect America Act of 2007	P.L. 110-55	121 Stat. 552	50 U.S.C. §1801 nt.	Provided authority for the Attorney General and the DNI to gather foreign intelligence information on persons believed to be overseas. The act expired in 2008.	
12/19/2007	Energy Independence and Security Act of 2007 (EISA)	P.L. 110-140	121 Stat. 1492	42 U.S.C. §§17381-17385	Gave NIST primary responsibility for developing interoperability standards for the electric-power "smart grid."	R41886
7/10/2008	Foreign Intelligence Surveillance Act of 1978 [FISA] Amendments Act of 2008	P.L. 110-261	122 Stat. 2436	See 50 U.S.C. §1801 nt. for affected provisions.	Added additional procedures to FISA (see p. 54) for acquisition of communications of persons outside the United States.	98-326
9/26/2008	Identity Theft Enforcement and Restitution Act of 2008	P.L. 110-326	122 Stat. 356	18 U.S.C. §1030	Authorized restitution to identity theft victims and modified some of the activities and penalties covered by 18 U.S.C. 1030.	R40599 97-1025
2/17/2009	Health Information Technology for Economic and Clinical Health Act	P.L. 111-5 (Title XIII of Div. A and Title IV of Div. B)	123 Stat. 226	42 U.S.C. §17901 et seq.	Expanded privacy and security requirements for protected health information by broadening HIPAA breach disclosure notification and privacy requirements to include business associates of covered entities.	R40546

Source: Various sources (see text), including National Research Council, *Toward a Safer and More Secure Cyberspace* (Washington, DC: National Academy Press, 2007); The White House, *Cyberspace Policy Review*, May 29, 2009, http://www.whitehouse.gov/assets/documents/Cyberspace_Policy_Review_final.pdf; and CRS.

Note: Prepared by Rita Tehan, Information Research Specialist (rtehan@crs.loc.gov, 7-6739) and Eric A. Fischer. Laws in *italics* are discussed in the text.

a. Office of the Law Revision Counsel, "United States Code Table of Classifications for Public Laws, 107th Congress, 1st Session (Covering Public Laws 107-1 through 107-136)," http://uscode.house.gov/classification/tbl107pl_1st.htm.

Author Contact Information

Eric A. Fischer
Senior Specialist in Science and Technology
efischer@crs.loc.gov, 7-7071

Acknowledgments

Contributing CRS staff include

- Patricia Moloney Figliola ("Communications Assistance for Law Enforcement Act of 1994"),

- Kristin M. Finklea ("Identity Theft and Assumption Deterrence Act of 1998," "Identity Theft Penalty Enhancement Act"),

- Wendy R. Ginsberg ("Freedom of Information Act (FOIA)," "Clinger-Cohen Act (Information Technology Management Reform Act) of 1996"),

- John Rollins ("Department of Defense Appropriations Act, 1987," "Intelligence Reform and Terrorism Prevention Act of 2004 (IRTPA)"),

- Kathleen Ann Ruane ("Antitrust Laws and Section 5 of the Federal Trade Commission Act"),

- Gina Stevens ("Electronic Communications Privacy Act of 1986"),

- Rita Tehan (Table 2), and

- Catherine A. Theohary ("Posse Comitatus Act of 1879," "U.S. Information and Educational Exchange Act of 1948 (Smith-Mundt Act)," and "Communications Decency Act of 1996").

www.ingramcontent.com/pod-product-compliance
Lightning Source LLC
Chambersburg PA
CBHW080534290526
45790CB00006B/2406